FOLLOWING FRANCIS

The Franciscan Way for Everyone

FOLLOWING FRANCIS

The Franciscan Way for Everyone

Susan Pitchford

MOREHOUSE PUBLISHING

Morehouse Publishing, P.O. Box 1321, Harrisburg, PA 17105

Morehouse Publishing, 445 Fifth Avenue, New York, NY 10016

Morehouse Publishing is an imprint of Church Publishing Incorporated.

Cover art: "Francis and the Wolf" by John August Swanson

Cover design: Corey Kent

Interior design: Carol Sawyer

Library of Congress Cataloging-in-Publication Data

Pitchford, Susan.
  Following Francis : the Franciscan way for everyone / Susan Pitchford.
     p. cm.
  Includes bibliographical references.
  ISBN-13: 978-0-8192-2235-0 (pbk.)
  1. Spiritual life—Catholic Church. 2. Secular Franciscan Order. 3. Francis, of Assisi,
Saint, 1182-1226. I. Title.
  BX3654.P58 2006
  255'.38—dc22

                              2006009593

Printed in the United States of America

07 08 09   10 9 8 7 6 5 4 3 2

To Crystal Bradford and Marilyn Brandenburg,
who taught me more than anyone else
what it means to be a Franciscan.

Contents

Acknowledgments

This is a book about being part of a community, and it certainly wasn't written in isolation. Three people were especially generous with their time and feedback: Edie Burkhalter, Wes Howard-Brook and Kim Pitchford. I might as well admit now that the debt I owe them will never be repaid. Fr. Allan Parker, my spiritual director, also read the manuscript as part of his general responsibility for keeping me on track. If there is any actual heresy in these pages, it's probably his fault. Fellow Franciscans who read early drafts include Dianne Aid, Barbara Baumgarten, Bill Berge, Crystal Bradford, Beverly Hosea and Adrienne Papermaster, and I am grateful for their impressions and insights. Marilyn Brandenburg read a draft and gave me her blessing shortly before her death in the fall of 2005; I remember her with deepest affection. Nancy Fitzgerald's enthusiasm for the project and her experience and expertise have made her the ideal editor for a first time author, and copyeditor Jennifer Hackett's encouragement and amazing eye have also been welcome gifts. Finally, my deepest thanks go to my husband Bob Crutchfield, who daily makes me grateful that I can follow Francis "in the world."

Preface

I'M STANDING IN A TINY ROOM carved out of the rock face of a cliff outside Assisi, looking down at the bed St. Francis slept on eight hundred years ago. My guidebook says that Francis liked an uncomfortable bed; feeling that time spent sleeping was time stolen from prayer, he liked to wake up often during the night. This tiny little bed, on which the great saint lay, would certainly do the trick: it's also carved out of the rock, and none too gently.

What a statement this ill-shapen little bed makes about Francis' passionate dedication to God. I, on the other hand, need my eight hours. I become cross when I don't get them—also stupid, which makes me more cross. Of course, Francis also fasted a lot, which is another discipline I have yet to master. Francis was a celibate, who made Lady Poverty his bride, whereas my husband and I make a living that is comfortable by American standards, outrageously luxurious by those of much of the world. Francis thought book learning made people susceptible to pride, and was suspicious of academics. I am a sociologist at a major university—though I confess that I am also suspicious of academics at times. Francis took Christ at his word when he said, "Sell all that you have, give to the poor, and come and follow me." He relinquished his ordinary life in the world to follow his master without distractions. I, on the other hand, live very much in the world, and constantly fight its seductions and demands.

And yet, I am a Franciscan. I am a member of the Third Order of the Society of St. Francis, the worldwide Anglican order for those who wish to live a Franciscan life without removing themselves from the world. "Third Orders" existed before Francis' time, and continue to offer Anglicans, Roman Catholics and others a way of living their Franciscan, Carmelite, Dominican or other vocation right where they are.[1] Other Franciscan Third Orders include the Secular Franciscan Order (Roman Catholic) and the Order of Ecumenical Franciscans. Third Order members, called "Tertiaries," are male and female, married and single, clergy and laity; some of us do "church work" for a living, but most of us have ordinary jobs. Francis himself founded the Third Order when Luchesio and Buonadonna, a husband and wife from Poggibonsi, wanted to share in his vision while remaining together as a couple. Francis set up the Order of Penance, which became the Third Order, and Pope Honorius III approved the Rule of the Order in 1221. Third Order Franciscans live a vowed life under a Rule with a set of definite components, flexible enough to accommodate people living in widely differing circumstances. What we all have in common is a deep commitment to following Jesus Christ, with Francis as our guide.

And so I am a Franciscan. An affluent, married, professional woman in twenty-first century America, I am trying to live according to a Rule established in the thirteenth century by an Italian religious fanatic barely five feet tall, and as medieval in mindset as he was in body. How this happened, and what it means to try to translate Franciscan spirituality into my own life and times, is what this book is about. It's organized around the nine elements of the Rule (Holy Eucharist, prayer, penitence, self-denial, simplicity, study, work, retreat and obedience), with additional chapters on other central Franciscan themes such as humility, chastity, love and joy. This book is very much the work of a newcomer to the Order, the story of someone encountering Francis for the first time. There are plenty of writers whose reflections on the Franciscan way have the mellow patina of maturity, and they are well worth reading.[2] What I've tried to do here is different: to show the beginnings of one Franciscan journey, being honest about both the joys and the struggles of that journey. It's a raw, unfinished and very personal story, and deliberately raises more questions than it answers. It's not a statement from the Order itself. I have no official position within the Order; I am only an ordinary member and am speaking only for myself.[3]

My objective is to speak to others who are where I was just a few years ago when this process began: wanting to go deeper in the spiritual life, and wanting the company of a community on the same path, but wondering where to begin. Affiliating with a religious order, whether as a full member or an associate or oblate, is one answer among many to that question. I suspect there are others for whom it might be a satisfying answer, too, if only they knew it existed, both in the Franciscan and other monastic traditions. This book is written for them, but also for those who are interested in exploring Franciscan spirituality on their own, as well as those who are attracted to the structure of a Rule of life based on the classical spiritual disciplines, whether linked to an existing order or not.

I wrote most of this book during a five-month period of extensive travel that included sabbatical stays in Cambridge, England, and Bellagio, Italy, as well as vacation time in Italy and Spain, a pilgrimage to Assisi, and field research in Western and Eastern Europe and Ghana. There is thus a sort of double-journey metaphor running through these pages. One of the benefits of travel is that it takes you out of your ordinary life and provides a change of background against which you can see familiar questions and struggles in fresh ways, bringing new issues to the surface. Because my field research involved visiting museums dedicated to historical atrocities, many of the places in which I wrote posed questions of their own—urgent, contemporary questions that Francis, even from a distance of eight hundred years, has helped me begin to answer.

I invite you as you read this book to discover what Francis has to say to you, and how a Franciscan perspective might help you deal with the questions and challenges in your own life. But I would especially invite you to experience something of Francis' passion. For Francis, to be a disciple of Jesus Christ was to be engaged in a lifelong love affair, swept into an intense dance with the Divine. It was a passionate God who called Francis into this dance, extending a torn hand in invitation. Everything that is distinctive and compelling about Francis' life followed directly from the intensity of this love: when Francis renounced worldly possessions, he did so that he might embrace the poor Christ unencumbered. And when he took the leper into his arms, the kiss he left on the disfigured face was given to the risen Lord.

It was this passion, and the exuberance with which he celebrated it, that drew me to Francis, and that I hope to pass on to you. Francis offers a spirituality of delight, and of a love that held onto that delight even in the midst of great suffering. Francis heard the call of Christ as an invitation to the divine dance, the steps marked out by the very Trinity, timed to the beating heart of God. He danced with a joy that drew people to him during his lifetime, and that still charms us today. I hope that in these pages, you will hear your own invitation to join in.

1

WHY FOLLOW FRANCIS?

One day . . . Friar Masseo desired to test how great [Francis']
humility was and went up to him and, as if in jest, said, "Why
after you? Why after you? Why after you?" Francis answered,
"What are you saying?" Friar Masseo said, "I say, why does all
the world follow after you, and why does every man seem to
desire to see you and to hear you and to obey you? You are not
a man beautiful of body, you are not greatly learned, you are not
noble: why then should all the world follow after you?" Hearing
this, St. Francis rejoiced greatly in spirit . . . and said, "Would
you know 'why after me'? Why all the world follows after me? I
have this from those eyes of the most high God, which in every
place behold the good and the wicked: namely, because those
most holy eyes have not seen among sinners any more vile, or
more insufficient, or a greater sinner than I am . . . [T]herefore,
He has chosen me to confound the nobility and the pride and
the strength and the beauty and wisdom of the world, so that it
may know that every virtue and every good thing is from Him. . . . "
—*The Little Flowers of St. Francis of Assisi, p. 24*[1]

IF IT WAS A MYSTERY TO MASSEO why people followed Francis during his lifetime, it's even more perplexing that people all over the
world are still following him eight hundred years later. Of course,

Francis is one of the most loved and admired saints the Church has ever produced, but it's one thing to admire a saint from a distance and quite another to take him as your model for the most important endeavor of your life. What makes people want to do this? There are really two questions here: first, what makes an otherwise ordinary person want to join a religious order at all—especially in mid-life, mid-career, even mid-marriage? Second, if a religious order at all, why Francis' order? All Franciscans have their own answers to these questions, of course, and I can only answer them with my own story.

After a decade-long hiatus following some painful experiences in the Church, I began to scratch and claw my way back to faith in the mid 1990s. As a freshman Christian I majored in penance, spending years in the phase the classical spiritual writers have called "purgation." Sunday after Sunday I wept my way through church, and on the days in between I wept some more. Luckily for me, the famous Anglican reserve held out and nobody bothered me too much, although they did make me welcome. I knew they meant it, but I also knew that I had no right to be there; I just kept coming back because there was no place else to go. I was supposed to be a "new creation," and my old self was supposed to pass away (2 Cor 5:17).[2] Yet my old self was not only alive, but positively athletic. At the same time, I was running into professional difficulties that beat up my ego even more. God was busy knocking every support out from under me, presumably so that I'd lean on him alone. I had some faith in this explanation, but it didn't diminish my sorrow, or my fear that God's patience was running out.

Then suddenly things began to change. Old attitudes and habits of thinking and acting dissipated, apparently without my doing anything much about them, and sorrow was increasingly displaced by joy. In short, God began liberating me from myself in his own good time. I felt like someone who's been knocking at a door for so long that she finally leans against it, exhausted, when it suddenly gives way and hurtles her headlong into the greatest party of all time. It's said that God's strength is made perfect in weakness (2 Cor 12:9), and I can at least say that I gave him ample opportunity to show off. Yet the more he did, the more isolated I felt. I imagine that many of the people in my parish have been through similar experiences, but no one ever seemed to talk about it. After-church coffee hour chat is superficial almost by definition, and adult classes, workshops and study groups all seemed to avoid getting too personal.

Occasionally there were glimpses of communities where people shared their spiritual journeys, but these communities didn't seem to be organized on the parish level. This makes sense, since most congregations are a mix of fresh-faced seekers and seasoned old saints, not to mention kids, young adults, couples, singles and ordinary screwed up folk. Unless the parish is a very large one, there's hardly a group to meet every need. I met one man whose community formed out of an ecumenical study group, but that seemed the sort of thing that either happens or it doesn't. Then I read Kathleen Norris's books describing her formation as a Benedictine oblate, and discovered that ordinary people could become attached to existing religious communities, and how much that experience had meant to her. It seemed an idea worth investigating. My parish happens to count among its members a Benedictine monk, who was willing to give me a crash course in religious orders and their different "styles."

I learned that Benedictines are specialists in moderation: "nothing harsh, nothing burdensome" as Benedict's famous Rule says. Their lives are centered around a disciplined schedule of prayer, study and work, and they are committed to the notion of balance—there's time in every day for the things that matter. They are also unique among monastic traditions in that they take a vow of stability, ordinarily staying put in the same house until death, though they may move as a matter of obedience. Stability, balance, moderation—I admire Benedictines, but I am not one of them.

The Trappists are an offshoot of the Benedictine Order, one of the reforms that went in the direction of a more stringent Rule. I mention them mainly because of the current popularity of "centering prayer," one of whose main spokesmen is a Trappist monk named Thomas Keating. Centering prayer is a method that involves sitting in silence for twenty minutes at a time, and using a "sacred word" chosen by the person as a means of dealing with intrusive thoughts. When thoughts interrupt the silence, you simply repeat the sacred word and let the thoughts float away. Centering prayer is big in these parts, and I've found the use of a sacred word to be an immensely helpful way of coping with distractions. But while I can see the value in having the pray-er maintain silence for the course of the sitting, I find it disturbing that, according to some of its proponents, this prayer also requires *God* to maintain silence throughout. I've put the question to several teachers of this method: What if God *wants* to speak, what am I supposed to do then? In each case, I was told to ignore anything that intrudes on the silence, that "if it's important, God will repeat it later when you can listen." Keating himself says, "Even if you see the heavens opening and Jesus sitting at the right hand of the Father, forget it. Return to the sacred word."[3] I don't know if all Trappists have the stones to tell the creator of the universe to keep quiet till their twenty minutes are up—maybe you get pretty tough when you follow a Rule as austere as theirs. But my frustration with centering prayer ended when I realized that of course Keating's approach would be rigid about silence: he's a *Trappist*, for God's sake. And I'm not.[4]

The Carmelites, on the other hand, understand the beauty and importance of silence without being rigid about it. I love Teresa of Avila's mix of radical devotion and relaxed openness: "If you want to make progress on the path and ascend to the places you have longed for, the important thing is not to think much but to love much, and so to do whatever best awakens you to love."[5] Indeed, I have learned so much from Teresa that she will be appearing often in this work, singing backup to Francis' lead. And I love another Carmelite, John of the Cross, as an answer to smiley-face Christians who preach that God wants us at all times to be healthy, wealthy and victorious. Still, all that talk of the desert did make me a bit nervous in my searching days, and I think I believed that if I didn't read about John's dark night of the soul, it might not happen to me. Fortunately, God is a lot smarter than I am, so it doesn't work that way. It wasn't until much later that I really came to appreciate Carmelite spirituality. Still, I was getting closer.

After going through all these monastic traditions, my Benedictine friend said, "And then there are the Franciscans, of course. They're . . . kind of . . . out there." *Perfect*, I thought. At last I have found the lunatic fringe of the Church. I like to tell people that I ended up with the Franciscans because they had the best website, but that's only partly true. The more I read about Francis, and Franciscan spirituality, the more I felt myself coming home. Unlike the Benedictine approach, the Franciscan way isn't balanced, moderate or stable, because Francis himself was none of those things. And while, like the Trappists, he spent much time silent before the Lord, Francis also loved to make up poetry and sing love songs to God. Francis believed there was a time to be silent, and a time to stick flowers in your hair and dance. And although Francis, like the Carmelites, was intimately acquainted with the desert, he could appreciate an oasis when he came across one as well.

Another thing that drew me to Franciscan spirituality was its dual emphasis. Like the beams of a cross, it has both a vertical and a horizontal dimension, stressing both contemplation and social justice. Franciscans seem especially attuned to the way the second great commandment is "like unto" the first: love of neighbor is *implied by* love for God, because our Lord likes to come to us disguised as our neighbor. Franciscans do not, of course, have a monopoly on this insight, but it was a central theme of Francis' own life, and is at the heart of the Franciscan way.

In the end, however, it was Francis the romantic who drew me onto this path. Francis' relationship with God was above all things *passionate*: he'd had that one good look at Jesus that leaves you weak in the knees, and ready to leave anything and everything behind to follow him. Francis understood that the God who is love (1 John 4:8) is also a "consuming fire" (Hebrews 12:29), and he spent his life being consumed by that love. Yet Francis understood passion in *both* its senses: his love wasn't just a rush of intense feelings, the spiritual joyride that is the goal of those we used to call "bliss ninnies." Francis' passion embraced the Cross along with the Crucified: he longed and prayed to share in Christ's suffering, a prayer that was generously answered.

Francis the romantic, the unbalanced and immoderate, the poet and contemplative, and the servant of the poor and outcast, provided me not only with a model and guide, but also with the community I'd been looking for. The St. Clare fellowship in Seattle became the place where I felt truly at home, because I was surrounded by people who didn't need an explanation: they already "got it." They understood the passion, they each had their own fanatic streak, and I could be as "out there" as I wanted, because they were all "out there" with me. The Third Order has given me a community small enough that we all know each other well, and yet the Order itself has similar communities on every continent. Francis wouldn't allow himself to be proud, of course. But I think Jesus is.

2

HOLY EUCHARIST
THE PASSION OF OUR GOD

The heart of [Tertiaries'] prayer is the Eucharist, in which they share with other Christians the renewal of their union with their Lord and Savior in his sacrifice, remembering his death and receiving his spiritual food.

—*The Principles of the Third Order of the Society of Saint Francis,* Day Fifteen[1]

HOW WOULD YOU CHOOSE TO SPEND the last night of your life? Jesus, knowing he was about to be betrayed by one friend, denied by another and abandoned by the rest, arrested, subjected to an unfair trial, tortured, humiliated and finally executed, paused to leave those same faithless friends a gift that ensured he'd be present to them until the end of time. The generosity of that gift, given by a soul in anguish at a time when the recipients least deserved it, is beyond comprehension. But Jesus had "loved his own who were in the world [and] he loved them to the end" (John 13:1). It was his passionate love for humankind that brought him into the world, and the force of that same love would cause him to "set his face" toward Jerusalem and the events of his own Passion.

It's no coincidence that the word "passion" connotes both love and suffering; indeed, these aren't so much two distinct meanings as two faces of the same experience. In a fallen world, love always contains an element of suffering, in part because our love always falls short of perfection. Human lovers, however much they long for it, can't achieve perfect union, which is why the greatest intimacy always contains an element of wistfulness. But also, the greater the love, the more fervent its desire to make the world perfect for the beloved, and the more frustrating its inability to do so. Christ, the incarnation of God's perfect love in the world, also embodied perfect suffering, and through that suffering he released us from the effects of sin so that we could rise with him to perfect union, and perfect joy. In this life, however, there is no perfection, and no separating love from suffering. So those who fall passionately in love with Christ, as Francis did, experience this tension at a new and more intense level, one that Teresa of Avila later described from her own experience:

> [The soul] is conscious of having been most delectably wounded, but cannot say how or by whom; but it is certain that this is a precious experience and it would be glad if it were never to be healed of that wound. . . . So powerful is the effect of this upon the soul that it becomes consumed with desire, yet cannot think what to ask, so clearly conscious is it of the presence of its God.[2]

The wound Teresa speaks of is the spiritual equivalent of an arrow to the chest: it may be painful, but removal means death, so you make friends with it. Francis would have welcomed this suffering in a way that would be foreign to most of us today. Steeped as he was in the medieval romantic tradition, he expected to endure heroic trials to please the one he loved. In *The Little Flowers of St. Francis of Assisi*, a collection of legends and stories about the saint gathered by an Italian Franciscan about a century after Francis' death, we read of Francis' zeal for the faith and his desire for martyrdom. In those days, the surest way to achieve that goal was to travel to the Muslim world and try your hand at evangelism. After a couple of failed attempts, Francis made it to Egypt, where he preached the gospel to the Sultan Malek al-Kamil. The Sultan was greatly moved by Francis' preaching, especially when Francis offered to jump into a fire together with the Sultan's holy men, and leave it to God to show whose faith was better. The Sultan didn't permit this, nor did he convert at that time, which would certainly have brought martyrdom to Francis and his companions as well as the sultan himself. Francis had to be content to go home in one piece, but he managed to find plenty of ordeals waiting for him within Christendom.

A longing for suffering and martyrdom is all but incomprehensible in our day, but to the medieval mind versed in the code of chivalry, a love that wasn't prepared to suffer was no love at all.[3] And if this were true of the knight's love for the unattainable lady, how much more so of the soul that participates in the love of Love itself. In her powerful book *The Passionate God*, Rosemary Haughton explains:

> [T]hose human beings who have even for a moment broken through to spheres of experience in which [Jesus] lived have suffered a longing for God so painful that it seemed, at times, that human nature could not support it. . . . There is no pain so great as the pain of the soul's longing for God. In it, all other pains are included and drawn to a point at which it is impossible to distinguish between pain and love. This is the urgency with which Jesus moved towards death, in the full impulse of passionate dedication.[4]

If all love involves suffering, how great must be the suffering of the one in love with God, who can neither see nor touch the object of his passion? And yet in the Eucharist, Christ has given us a way to see and touch him, a way to experience his embrace. While perfect union with God can't be realized in this life, our Lord in his compassion gave us something to hold onto. Francis held on for all he was worth, and he advised his followers to do the same:

> [Christ] shows himself to us in this sacred bread just as he once appeared to his apostles in real flesh. With their own eyes they

saw only his flesh, but they believed that he was God, because they contemplated him with the eyes of the spirit. We, too, with our own eyes, see only bread and wine, but we must see further and firmly believe that this is his most holy Body and Blood, living and true.[5]

Francis' devotion to the Eucharist was so great that he made every effort to attend Mass daily and receive communion frequently, and he counseled his friars to do the same,[6] though the practice wasn't common in those days. He urged priests of his Order to celebrate Mass with the greatest reverence, and lay brothers to regard both priest and sacrament with the same awe that transported him:

> Our whole being should be seized with fear, the whole world should tremble and heaven rejoice, when Christ the Son of the living God is present on the altar in the hands of the priest. What wonderful majesty! What stupendous condescension! O sublime humility! O humble sublimity! That the Lord of the whole universe, God and the Son of God, should humble himself like this and hide under the form of a little bread, for our salvation.[7]

Annie Dillard is one contemporary writer who gets this:

> Does anyone have the foggiest idea of what sort of power we so blithely invoke? Or, as I suspect, does no one believe a word of it? . . . It is madness to wear ladies' straw hats and velvet hats to church; we should all be wearing crash helmets. Ushers should issue life preservers and signal flares; they should lash us to our pews.[8]

A Franciscan friend of mine says that going from Eucharist to coffee hour is like jumping through a plate glass window, and I think Francis would agree. Francis, who longed to be one with Christ, understood that in this sacrament we do achieve union with him, on a level so profound we may not have access to it.

That is to say, we may not be consciously aware of anything much happening. But whether we "feel" anything or not, in the Eucharist Christ communicates himself to us. "[T]hrough him was life" (John 1:4), and it is through the sacrament of his body and blood that this life animates us (John 6:53–54). While Francis experienced the suffering inherent in a passionate longing for God, in the Eucharist he could be consoled by the knowledge that his longing was the responding echo of God's own passion for him.

In writing of the passion of God for us, Haughton begins with the premise that since humans bear the image of God, we can learn a lot about how God loves us by observing how humans love one another. This is why the Eucharist always reminds me of sex. And no, my mind doesn't wander *that* much in church. But in the context of a loving, committed relationship, there is no greater intimacy than that which occurs when bodies bring souls into contact. By this same principle, when our bodies encounter the body and blood of Christ, soul and spirit meet as well, and become one. So the Eucharist is to the spiritual life what sex is to romantic relationships, and perhaps this is why St. Paul issued such grave warnings about the danger of receiving the Eucharist "in an unworthy manner" (1 Cor 11:27–30): like sex divorced from love, it loses its intended meaning and becomes distorted and even harmful.

The Eucharist is analogous to sex not only in serving as a focus of intimacy, but in the way it defines the entire relationship. This struck me vividly in Paris a few years ago, when my husband, his daughter and mother and I were visiting the Cathedral of Notre Dame. It's a powerful place; as my husband observed at the time, "Anyone could get religion in here." We wandered around being tourists, and then came upon a Mass being said at one of the altars. I experienced a sudden, intense desire to vault over the railing and join them, but this wouldn't have been popular with the rest of my party, nor, I suspect, with the officials charged with maintaining order in the cathedral. I moved away, saddened at first, until I realized that it didn't matter that much that I wasn't receiving the sacrament at that moment, because I am *among those who do.*

Married people don't spend every waking moment having sex, after all. But the fact that their relationship is a sexual one defines it and creates expectations about it, both on the part of the couple, and among their family and friends, as well as society itself. In our culture, people in this kind of relationship are expected to be monogamous and loyal, not to humiliate their partner before others, to come to their partner's aid in times of trouble, and to at least feign an interest in the trivial events of the other's day. What it comes down to is that having a license to sleep with someone brings with it certain expectations, which is why sexual relationships that don't involve a license are so much more work: the expectations aren't always clear, and much additional negotiation must take place. Even there, however, couples in a sexual relationship are expected at the very least to leave the party together. Likewise, we who are "Eucharistic people" stand in a particular relationship to Christ: we are his intimates, made one with him and with each other in his body. Because we "know" him, we are known as his, and that colors everything else about us.

This is why the *Principles of the Third Order* place the Eucharist at the "heart" of our prayer: it's the intimacy that forms the core of our relationship to Christ. We're called to participate "frequently": at a minimum, on Sundays and major feast days. Ideally, the Eucharist is celebrated at Third Order fellowship meetings, but this is not possible for every fellowship. Beyond this, it's up to the individual to determine what "frequent" participation means. Just before entering the formation program, I began attending a mid-week Mass each week and have incorporated this into my Rule. It's a luxury I guard jealously; colleagues, teaching assistants and students are told that I have a standing meeting off campus at that time, and am unavailable for anything else. I expect they think I'm meeting with a shrink, or a support group for sex addicts, but it doesn't really matter. That "meeting" time is literally sacred and virtually non-negotiable, though if I really can't make it, I know the mid-week Eucharist schedules of several other parishes in my area where I can make it up. In the five years since I've made this practice a priority, I've felt the truth of Jesus' words: "By eating my flesh and drinking my blood you enter into me and I into you" (John 6:56, *The Message*).

The greatest obstacle to frequent participation in the Eucharist for Episcopalians is that our churches don't tend to offer it as often as Roman Catholic churches do, which can present difficulties for those whose schedules aren't so flexible. Many Protestant churches, of course, offer communion even less frequently: weekly, monthly or even quarterly. There are those who prefer it this way, feeling that receiving more often would make the experience less "special," and of course these differences also reflect a different understanding of what is happening during communion. In my corner of the Church, we believe along with Francis that Christ is truly present in what was once ordinary bread and wine. This explains Francis' desire to meet the One he loved there as often as possible. My own preference would be to receive daily— not because I'm such a holy person, but because I can only hold my breath for so long.

Ultimately, there's nothing we can say about the Eucharist that isn't wholly inadequate. It is like trying to describe God himself: words stumble over each other, and either become poetry or gibberish. Francis, God's troubadour, produced more poetry than most. But every now and then we get a glimpse of him being awed toward the limits of language, and it's there that his own passion shines most brightly:

> May the power of your love, Lord Christ, fiery and sweet as honey, wean my heart from all that is under heaven, so that I may die for love of your love, who were so good as to die for love of my love. Amen. (*The Absorbeat*, attributed to St. Francis)

Questions for Reflection

1. Where in your life do you see love mingled with suffering? What does it mean to "love someone till it hurts"? Is there anyone you love that way, and if so, where does the "hurt" come from?

2. What is your understanding of what occurs during the Holy Eucharist? In what sense is Christ "present" there? How does he "communicate" himself to us through the sacrament and give us life?

3. Are there times when you're especially eager or especially reluctant to receive Holy Communion? What factors affect your feelings about it?

4. How often do you receive? Does your church tend to celebrate it more or less often? Do you feel a desire to receive more often, or are you concerned that frequent participation might make it less "special"?

5. Do you have any special way of preparing to receive Christ in the Eucharist? If not, how might you make yourself ready for this special meeting?

Steps into Eucharist

1. Christ is "really present" to us in the Eucharist, but how often are we "really present" to him? The next time you participate in the liturgy, make a special effort to be fully present and attentive. Notice its structure, how we are prepared for the culminating moment through the ministry of the Word and through prayer and silence. How does it feel to worship "with angels and archangels and all the company of heaven"?

2. It's easier to participate fully in the Eucharist if we understand what's going on. Educate yourself on the sacrament. Churches will sometimes offer an "instructed Eucharist," pausing to explain the meaning of each part of the liturgy as they go. An excellent instructed Eucharist can also be found online at: http://www.metanoia.org/martha/writing/instructed.htm. Another helpful resource is Tom Wright's book *The Meal Jesus Gave Us* (Louisville: Westminster John Knox Press, 2003), a short and easy to understand but very compelling reflection on the Eucharist.

3. Experiment with receiving Holy Communion at a time when you normally wouldn't. That is, if you normally receive on

Sundays, try attending a mid-week service. If you're a member of a church that only celebrates Eucharist once a month or less, you might visit a church one Sunday where it's celebrated weekly. Or it might be preferable to visit a mid-week service so as not to miss worship in your own community. All baptized Christians are welcome to receive communion in Episcopal churches.

4. Reflect on how it feels to seek out this means of intimacy with Christ more often. Does it nourish you? Do you feel you're in danger of taking it for granted? Listen attentively to Christ's call to you in this area: does he seem to be drawing you in one direction or the other?

Prayer

Lord Jesus, in the Eucharist you have given us the precious gift of yourself. In this, the holiest of acts, you enter into us and we into you. Give us a zealous desire to meet you and each other at your table, and to know you in the breaking of the bread. Amen.

3

PRAYER
OCEAN POURING INTO OCEAN

Tertiaries seek to live in an atmosphere of praise and prayer. They aim to be constantly aware of God's presence, so that they may indeed pray without ceasing. . . . Tertiaries recognize the power of intercessory prayer for furthering the purposes of God's kingdom, and therefore seek a deepening communion with God in personal devotion, and constantly intercede for the needs of his church and his world. Those who have much time at their disposal give prayer a large part in their daily lives. Those with less time must not fail to see the importance of prayer and to guard the time they have allotted to it from interruption.

—*The Principles of the Third Order of the Society of Saint Francis,* Days Fourteen and Sixteen.[1]

JUST AS MARRIED PEOPLE DON'T SPEND every waking moment having sex, Christians don't spend their whole lives at the altar receiving the Eucharist. It takes up, in fact, a relatively small share of our time—quite out of proportion to its significance. Meanwhile, there's a whole relationship to be conducted outside those moments of greatest intimacy, which weaves that intimacy into the rest of our life, and the communication through which we conduct this relationship is prayer.

There is no specifically Franciscan method of prayer. Unlike many of the masters of prayer throughout the history of the Church, Francis didn't develop or teach a system of prayer techniques for his followers—he seems to have been too busy praying.[2] Instead, it's his general orientation to prayer that Francis is known for: he was a man immersed in "the spirit of prayer and holy devotion."[3] St. Bonaventure, who composed Francis' biography in the years following his death, wrote of the saint's devotion to prayer:

> [H]e tried to keep his spirit always in the presence of God, by praying to him without intermission, so that he might not be without some comfort from his Beloved. . . . Whether he was walking or sitting, at home or abroad, whether he was working or resting, he was so fervently devoted to prayer that he seemed to have dedicated to it not only his heart and his soul, but all his efforts and all his time.[4]

Francis didn't chronicle his prayer life in the way of Teresa of Avila or Mechtilde of Magdeburg, so we have little direct knowledge of what passed between him and God when he prayed. But from the observations of his companions (who apparently ignored his orders to stay away when he was praying), we know that when Francis retreated to solitary places to be alone with God, he experienced that Presence with a passionate intensity.

Francis' spiritual "style" was deeply contemplative, but for him contemplation never implied withdrawal from the world, or from active service.[5] Because he so profoundly integrated the active and contemplative dimensions, the Franciscan way has been described as "contemplative action," in which the fruit of ceaseless prayer is ceaselessly offered to the world.[6] Stare at any bright light long enough, and you'll continue to see that light everywhere you look. It was this that enabled Francis to embrace the lepers he'd once turned from in disgust: he simply went on seeing Christ when he looked at them.

The schedule of prayers Francis established for his friars provided generously for both corporate and solitary prayer, both formal liturgy and adoration. For Tertiaries in our time, the particulars have changed but the principle remains, because relationships still take time and work. Just as married couples discuss everything from paying the bills to their common history and their dreams for the future, so Tertiaries are expected to share the full spectrum of their lives with God, from their most exalted longings to their most prosaic concerns. The wisdom of the Rule is in providing for both, and the basic structure that supports our prayer is the Daily Office. These ancient services are based in the monastic tradition in which communities, including the earliest Franciscans, have for centuries gathered at intervals throughout the day and night to pray.[7] The Book of Common Prayer boiled these down to the two Offices of morning and evening prayer.[8] Each contains prayers of confession, petition and intercession, praise, thanksgiving and oblation (the offering of oneself to God), all forms of prayer expected of Tertiaries. Francis composed some beautiful prayers for his followers, many of which can be incorporated into the Office, such as these simple words of praise: "You are good, all good, the highest good, the only good."[9] Each Office also includes a set of Scripture readings, with a special emphasis on the Psalms.

All Tertiaries in the Province of the Americas are expected to recite at least one of these Offices each day. Although this same expectation is placed on all clergy in the Episcopal Church, it's probably not a familiar discipline to most lay people—certainly it wasn't to me—and it can take a bit of getting used to. Outside the context of the Eucharist, I'm not typically drawn to the recitation of set prayers, and I know I'm not alone in having to fight against boredom when saying the same prayers every day for years on end. But the secret of the Office is the same as any other discipline: while it may be difficult, monotonous and downright irritating at times, the more you give yourself to it, the more it gives back to you. As a child I took piano lessons, and like most kids, I loathed the daily practice. Most kids probably don't take it out on the piano itself, but my parents' piano still has the marks just above the keyboard where I bent over one day and bit it. I mean, I bit the *wood*. And because I bit the piano instead of practicing it, I can't sit down today and express myself through music, like the kids who kept at it.

Spiritual disciplines are no different: if you stick with them through the hard and boring parts, they'll eventually reward you, and this is as true of the Daily Office as it is of fasting, meditation or solitude. All prayer lives have their rhythms I suppose, and I experience mine as alternating between time in the desert and time at the oasis, times of extreme aridity in which God seems a million miles away, and times when he's so near I could almost forget to breathe. There's a sort of middle ground I think of as the "prairie"—neither desert nor oasis, but a state in which God is available if I'm paying attention. At the oasis, when God is fanning me with palm fronds and dropping dates into my mouth, it's easy to look down on the Office as a boring, pedestrian form of prayer. But it's in the desert where the Office comes into its own. At those times I can hardly pray at all; I feel like I'm talking to myself, just going through the motions. But I've found that when you're just going through the motions, it's immensely helpful to have motions to go through. So in the periods of aridity, it's the Office that enables me to keep praying, to just keep saying the familiar words, and trust that they'll form a bridge over the chasm opening up beneath me. I've learned from John of the Cross not to fear those dark, lonely periods, because it turns out that the darkness itself is filled with God. But I couldn't have held out long enough to come to that understanding without the structure of the Office to support me.

Francis knew better than to turn up his nose at "pedestrian" forms of prayer. A story is told that a bishop once paid Francis a visit, when he was living in a hermitage in the wilderness. As they walked around the grounds, however, the bishop noticed that the little hut was surrounded by beautiful gardens. He asked Francis how he was able to keep the gardens so lovely, and Francis replied, "Prayer." Surprised, the bishop said, "You mean you just pray, and God takes care of your gardens?" "No," Francis answered, "I pray with a hoe." Now this is largely a lesson about the relationship of prayer to action—*laborare est orare*—("to work is to pray," as the Benedictines say), but I also find it moving to think of the great saint communing with God through hours spent simply scraping away at the earth. In his humility, Francis would have understood and accepted that it's in the daily plugging away at ordinary tasks—including ordinary prayers—that we draw near to God.

Again, the comparison with romantic relationships is instructive. In the beginning, couples spend most of their time together doing "special" things: dining out, going to the theater, attending concerts and the like. But it's when you find yourself with your beloved in the plumbing aisle at Home Depot that you know things are serious. Likewise, it's when we stop "dating" God just on Christmas and Easter, or even just on Sundays, and invite him into the ordinary tasks of ordinary days that we know the relationship is getting serious. And to do this, we need to pray ordinary prayers: petition, intercession, thanksgiving and so on. Knowing this, Francis' life included both the prayer of everyday business and the everyday business of prayer—both the mundane concerns of human existence and the discipline of staying with it day after day, year after year.

And yet, it's possible to carry this emphasis on the "ordinary" too far. It's become so fashionable to talk about finding God in the ordinary that we run the risk of forgetting that, as Christians, our lives aren't supposed to be so ordinary that they're indistinguishable from everyone else's. The emphasis on the ordinary is undoubtedly a healthy corrective to the bliss ninnies who thrive on spiritual exotica and want all the elation without the work. But as C. S. Lewis wisely observed, if a man fell off the right side of his horse the last time, you can be sure that next time he'll fall off the left. I can easily see Francis praying with a hoe, but I also have another picture in my mind. There's a sculpture in the grounds of one of Francis' hermitages outside Assisi[10] that shows the saint in ecstasy, supine on the ground. Francis knew what it was to share with God the minutiae, the boredom and the petty concerns of life. But he didn't become absorbed in them: he was absorbed in

God. He wasn't so busy with his hoe that he forgot to look up and be swept away by God's glory.

There's another story about Francis' practice of prayer that's recounted in *The Little Flowers*.[11] Once, before Francis had begun to attract followers, he was invited to dinner by Bernard of Quintavalle, one of the principal citizens of Assisi. Bernard was curious about this man who was already gaining some attention in the town, so he often invited Francis to his home to observe him, and test his sincerity. On this occasion they talked late into the night, and upon retiring both men immediately pretended to be asleep, Bernard snoring loudly. Soon Bernard saw Francis rise quietly and kneel to pray. He remained caught up in prayer the entire night, repeating again and again, "My God and my all!" The next day Bernard renounced his possessions and became a follower of Francis, who throughout his life gave himself to intense and concentrated periods of prayer in which some mighty strange things were known to happen.

Francis is clearly hiking above the timberline here, and the prospect of trying to follow him can be intimidating. How do we begin? This is not the place, and I am not the person, to provide detailed instruction on prayer. But wherever we do get our instruction, and whatever methods we follow, there are a few virtually universal challenges people face in learning to pray, and some very basic principles that help us meet those challenges.

The first is that if we're serious about our relationship with God, and serious about learning to pray, we need to make a serious commitment of time to it. Like Christ, Francis frequently paused from active service and withdrew to remote places to be alone with God. He established a collection of hermitages where he and his brothers could pray in seclusion, and he spent about half the year in solitude.[12] Very few of us living a Franciscan vocation "in the world" can accompany Francis this far, but we should remember what Jesus said of the widow's mite: it's not how much we give, but how much we give of what we have to give, that counts. Those of us with families, jobs and ministries can't disappear for months at a time, but if we want to experience spiritual growth, we'll have to make prayer a priority.

How much time that means will vary from one person to the next, and it can also vary from one season to the next. The rhythms of the academic year mean that my life also alternates between periods of intensive service and slower times that have more room for prayer. If we can identify these rhythms in our lives, we can avoid having the busy times push us to panic when we can't get alone as much as we'd like, knowing that we're in the best of company. The Third Order Rule recognizes that how much time we can give to prayer depends on our circumstances. As with our monetary giving, however, we'll know we've made a start when our time commitment makes us a bit nervous. I first began to sense that I'd grown serious about prayer when I realized that my prayer time was going to cost me a promotion. That may not be the standard for you—God may *want* you to be promoted—but if the time you spend in prayer doesn't require some level of sacrifice, you may need to re-think your level of commitment.

Second, once we've set aside the time and said our prayers of confession, petition, intercession, thanksgiving and whatever others we may be led to say, we need to stop talking. This may seem incredibly obvious, or it may not. Luckily for me, my parents never taught me to "say my prayers," so I didn't have to get over the idea that prayer consists of me presenting God with a list of errands, and then walking away. This doesn't strike me as the best way to form a close relationship; in fact, having fallen in love several times in my life, I can't recall a single time when it happened like that. Mostly the pattern has been a good bit of conversational to-and-fro, and then quiet, rather heated, togetherness. Prayer, too, passes from dialogue to silent, attentive delight, from asking to adoration. The Curé d'Ars (a French saint and Tertiary who died in 1859) met a peasant in church once, who practiced a very simple but profound method of prayer: "I look at him, and he looks at me."[13] Anyone who's been in love knows that the look exchanged between lovers is a powerful thing; in Charles Williams' words, it is "ocean pouring into ocean and itself receiving ocean."[14]

Third, something must be done about the fact that, for most of us, trying to be silent in the presence of God feels very much like being trapped inside a pinball machine. Ping! What am I making for dinner? Ping! When am I going to get that review done? Ping! I wonder if the dog needs to go out? It's probably good for the over-inflated ego to discover how little control we have over our own thought processes, but it can be sorely frustrating. Teachers of prayer have known this forever, which is why they've developed a wide variety of ways to deal with it, including the rosary, prayer ropes, mantras, a "sacred word," walking a labyrinth, weaving a basket or knitting an afghan. The method doesn't matter much, so long as we have something to which we can anchor our restlessness. When our restless minds and bodies are given some task to focus on, then our spirits can quiet down and be available to God. *I look at him, and he looks at me.* And while it's useful to experiment with different methods until we find one that works for us, it's important then to settle into that method, and not flit around from the rosary to the Jesus prayer to something else.

Fourth, when we're ready to be attentive to God, most of us find that we need a "way in" to prayer. That is, even when our minds have been stilled, we still need something to draw us into the presence of God, and the masters of prayer have known this, too. *Lectio divina* (sacred reading) is one way of doing this, in which a short passage of Scripture or some other spiritual reading is read slowly and attentively, allowing the words to sink in. Then you meditate on the passage, allowing God to speak through it to you. Finally, you allow the meditation to lead you into prayer. I learned a sort of amateur *lectio* as a teenager and practiced it for years before I ever heard the term, and I can vouch for its usefulness. This isn't the reading that one does for study, to analyze the text; rather, it's to allow the text to become in a sense a "living word" that God speaks directly to you. Music can be another very effective way into prayer; indeed, I've found that certain pieces can actually become prayer, and I can "pray" the same two songs over and over again for months. Music like this never fails to capture my wandering attention, and redirect it to God. Icons are yet another way into prayer. There are some excellent books on how to pray with icons, and I've found certain films, especially that rare thing, a really well done life of Christ,[15] to be extremely useful as "moving icons" that invite me into the presence of God.

To stop talking, to anchor our restlessness, and to find a way into prayer: these are all important things for us to do, if we want to draw closer to God. But the greatest teachers of prayer tell us there's a point where our efforts in prayer cease and God takes over. This is a principle that also applies to the spiritual disciplines more generally. The disciplines of Eucharist, study, penitence, retreat and so on that make up the Franciscan Rule are not things we do to transform ourselves; rather, they are our way of putting ourselves in a position where God can effect the transformation.[16] As with surgery, the patient is responsible for showing up and getting on the table, but the real work will be done by the surgeon. And what is true for the disciplines in general is doubly true for prayer: if we stay faithful to the practices we know, and do what we can, a time will come when God will do what we can't. Teresa of Avila, Evelyn Underhill[17] and many others have described this moment as an early step toward contemplation, and the point where the soul progresses not through its own efforts, but by the direct action of God.

This may or may not be accompanied by any conscious experience of the nearness of God—"consolations," as Teresa would have said. It's important to recognize that many lifelong contemplatives never experience any particular pleasure in prayer, and those who carry on for years without such encouragement must be a great delight to God. I need to avoid the temptation to be mercenary in my relationship to him; although he's patient with the mixed bag of motives I bring, ultimately I want to love him for himself, and not for the gifts he can give. Yet there are some contemporary teachers of prayer who so downplay the gifts that I think they're in danger of insulting the Giver. I think of a father who comes home from a business trip with gifts for his children. Obviously he doesn't want to be greeted by a gaggle of brats whose first utterance is, "What did you bring me?" But surely he would be disappointed if, having greeted him properly, they scorned the gifts altogether. One spiritual director advised Teresa of Avila to meet any vision of Christ with a rude gesture, which caused her great suffering. She complained often and with feeling about overly timid, unimaginative confessors who were scared senseless by the smallest sign that God might actually be alive and have something to say.

There are those who have been socialized into such mistrust of emotions that the "exuberant mysticism"[18] of Teresa is deeply suspect—let alone the romantic or frankly erotic mysticism of Bernard of Clairvaux, Marguerite Porète, Mechtilde of Magdeburg, Hadewijch of Brabant, Beatrijs of Nazareth and their ilk.[19] Probably because of his immersion in the medieval romantic tradition, Francis seems very much at ease with lavish expressions and experiences of love for God: "[W]hen the saint was alone in prayer, he would give free rein to his emotions: laughing one minute and crying the next, singing mystical love songs in French at the top of his lungs one instant, and praying in hushed silence the next."[20]

Francis' perseverance through times of deep spiritual darkness and near despair shows that there was nothing mercenary about his love. But he was a man whose spiritual life was filled with delight, and he accepted both the songs of birds and of angels as gifts from God. What kept both Francis and Teresa safe from deception through the unusual experiences they had in prayer was that they were both steeped in the Scriptures, and they were both always under spiritual direction. They knew the written word of God well enough to know if it were being contradicted, which would have been grounds for immediate dismissal of anyone trying to pose as an angel of light.[21] And their prayer lives were always subjected to the discernment of their confessors—a crucial protection against going off spiritually half-cocked. A wise spiritual director will examine our experiences in light of the fruit being borne in our lives,[22] knowing that the smallest act of charity outweighs a dozen visions: as a line from *Les Misérables* puts it, "To love another person *is* to see the face of God." It is impossible to overstate the importance of these protections, simply because we are capable of filling our own minds with the most absurd notions, and flattering ourselves that we are spiritually "advanced." And yet to close ourselves off completely from the work of God in our hearts is merely to fall off the other side of the horse.

There is no specifically Franciscan method of prayer. But it seems safe to say that prayer is more Franciscan in style when it is characterized by the central traits of Franciscan spirituality: humility, love and joy. Franciscans are driven to prayer by a deep sense of inner poverty: "My soul thirsteth for thee, my flesh longeth for thee in a dry and thirsty land, where no water is" (Psalm 63:1, KJV). This poverty is by no means cringing or shameful, but delights in our dependence on one who delights in giving. Our prayer is also passionate; we are drawn to Christ because we are, in Goethe's words, "insane for the light."[23] And our prayer is joyous, in the deepest sense: it relishes the best wine at the wedding feast, but it also welcomes the cross when it comes. This is because, as the *Principles of the Third Order* remind us, "Jesus calls those who would serve him to follow his example and choose for themselves the same path of renunciation and sacrifice. *To those who hear and obey he promises union with God"* (The Principles of the Third Order of the Society of Saint Francis, Day Three; my emphasis).

It is this union that is the goal of all that we do as Christians, both our prayer and our active service. When I was newly returned to the faith, I used to think of heaven as *A Place Where.* A place where bodies would always work properly, and never break down. A place where all one's little neuroses would be cured. A place where everyone would have a house on the beach, and there would be no sharks in the water. In short, a place where all problems would be solved, and everything would be perfect. But there does come a time to put away childish things, and I now see that heaven is not a place at all, but a Person. People more grown-up than I have talked about the "beatific vision," and this begins to make sense to me now: *I look at him, and he looks at me.* When my mother-in-law was dying, I sat by her bedside one day and we speculated a bit about what was to come. I told her I believe that when I see the face of Christ, every desire and every longing I've ever had will be satisfied. She closed her eyes, nodded and whispered, "Yes." I understand now that heaven is not A Place Where. Heaven is being in God—together with the whole communion of saints—and hell is not being in God. In prayer, when we are graced with a foretaste of that union, it is like rain falling into water: sometimes with a great splash, sometimes softly, but always plunging in and becoming one. Ocean pouring into ocean, and itself receiving ocean: I look at him, and he looks at me.

Questions for Reflection

1. What are some of the challenges and frustrations you experience in prayer? When has prayer not been challenging or frustrating? What do you think made the difference?

2. Are there certain times when you find it especially easy or hard to pray? Are there places that are especially conducive to prayer, or places where you find it difficult to pray?

3. What are the rhythms of your prayer life? Do you experience periods when prayer comes easily, and periods when it's difficult or impossible to pray? If so, how do you respond when God seems far away?

4. How has your practice of prayer, or your relationship with God, evolved over time? Do you see changes in the types of prayers you pray, in the time you spend in prayer, in the depth of your prayer life? How have these changes come about?

5. Is there anything in your life that seems to be impeding your prayer? Grudges, addictions, apathy, self-loathing and a host of other things can make us feel "stalled" on our way to God. How might you deal with things in your life that have become barriers between you and God?

6. Francis exemplified "contemplative action," the creative synthesis of prayer and service in the world. How do these two elements come together in your life? Do you feel a call to be more attentive to one or the other? How might you begin to explore this call?

Steps into Prayer

1. Start by setting aside a time and place each day to be alone with God, and show up. Put it in your calendar if you need to, and make it *good* time—not the bits of the day that are left over when everyone else has taken their piece. Don't be over-ambitious; if you start with the kind of schedule Francis kept, you'll give up before the first day is out. But do make a commitment that will stretch you a little.

2. Look for "dead time" in your day that you can reclaim for prayer. Time spent commuting to work, riding the elevator or waiting in line can either be a nuisance or an opportunity to touch base with God.

3. Test drive the Daily Office. If you don't have a Book of Common Prayer, you can find both morning and evening prayer online at www.tssf.org. Experiment with saying an Office each day for a week; how does it feel to introduce this kind of structure into your prayer life? Once you know the Office by heart, you can say it in the shower, walking the dog or doing the dishes—more "dead time" reclaimed.

4. In addition to your regular list of intercessions, trying "praying the news": offer prayers for the lost children, the victims of crime and natural disasters, the leaders of the world and those whose lives they affect. Experiment also with short prayers for the people you encounter during your day: a lonely neighbor, a worried-looking rider on the bus, a coworker who's going through a tough time.

5. To keep returning to prayer throughout the day, make a habit of starting each new task with a prayer. I keep it simple: when I pick up a stack of exams or sit down to respond to students' email, I cross myself and say, "To the glory of God and in the name of the Father, and of the Son, and of the Holy Spirit. Amen." As I head to class, I pray: "Let the words of our mouths and the meditation of our hearts be acceptable in your sight, oh Lord our strength and our redeemer." These prayers don't take a lot of time or thought; they're a kind of shorthand for my standing

request that my work might be acceptable to God, that he would make up for its deficiencies, and use it to accomplish some good in the world.

6. If distractions during prayer are a problem, experiment with praying while doing some repetitive motion. Running or walking, knitting, washing dishes and weeding the garden are all ways of anchoring our restlessness so our spirits can be still. You might also want to try such time-honored techniques as the rosary. Uncomfortable with Hail Marys? Try the Anglican rosary (see www.franciscan.org.au/anglicanrosary.html), or any string of beads. Choose any short prayer you like; the Psalms are a good place to begin (I like the rhythm of Ps. 63:1: "My soul thirsteth for thee, my flesh longeth for thee").

7. Try *lectio divina* as a way of praying the Scriptures. Choose a text and read it slowly several times, attentive for any word, phrase or image that seems to speak to you. Then sit quietly with it, and allow it to draw you more deeply into God's presence, until you can rest in the silence together. Again, the Psalms are particularly suitable for this (try Psalm 27, or 139), as are the gospel narratives. Lectio divina can also be practiced with any spiritual reading, with music or with nature. A friend of mine can spend hours with a tide pool; once you develop the habit of looking for them, you'll see God's invitations everywhere.

8. Try sitting still and returning Jesus' gaze. Look at him, while he looks at you. See your image in his eyes; do you look different there from the way you habitually see yourself? Start small—if you're not practiced at adoration, try it for five minutes. You may find it helpful to begin by focusing on an icon of Christ. Tired of blond-haired, blue-eyed Christs? See www.bridge building.com for images of Jesus with a refreshing bit of color.

9. Finally, don't forget to pray in community. The next time you're praying with a group, notice how it feels to join your prayer to theirs. There is a special power in praying as part of the body of Christ. Francis recognized this, and made corporate prayer a significant part of his life. We should not fail to do the same.

Prayer

Oh God, you have searched me and known me. You inhabit the desert and the oasis, the darkness and the light. You inhabit the praise of your people, our highest joy and our deepest pain. Kindle in my heart the fire of Francis' passion, so that I too will search and know you, in your creation and in the least of your brothers and sisters. Amen.

4

LOVE
EROS IS ONE OF GOD'S NAMES

Let him kiss me with the kisses of his mouth; for thy love is
better than wine.

—Song of Songs 1:2, KJV

Love is the distinguishing feature of all true disciples of Christ
who wish to dedicate themselves to him as his servants.

—*The Principles of the Third Order of the Society
of Saint Francis,* Day Twenty-Five

MY FAMILY TOOK A TRIP in celebration of love: specifically, my parents' fiftieth anniversary. We decided to revisit the two places we had lived abroad, so after a month of work in northern Italy, my husband and I joined my parents and my sister for a week in Rome and a week in Seville. One of the great benefits of having lived in a place is that when you return, you don't feel any great obligation to see the sights; you can just settle in and enjoy the things you like best about it. We didn't need to "do" the Coliseum, and we could see the dome of St. Peter's from our terrace. But when my mother happened to read a passage in her guidebook about Bernini's famous sculpture *The Ecstasy of Saint Teresa of Avila,* I decided that seeing that sculpture was the one thing I really wanted to do in Rome.

It took us four tries: the first time, we went to the wrong church, having misread the directions. The second time, we mistook the church next door for the right one, a fact we only discovered when, after much pleading, the man at the door agreed to let us in for two minutes after closing. When we realized our mistake, we hurried to the right church—Santa Maria della Vittoria—which had just closed. Finally, the next day, we got it right, and Bernini's genius more than justified the effort. Teresa is depicted in a sort of swoon: head back, eyes closed, lips parted. Above her is an angel with an arrow aimed at her heart. A window high overhead sends light down a set of gold rays, so that the incoming sunlight bathes them in a golden glow. My mother's guidebook describes the sculpture as "highly theatrical and sexually ambiguous. . . . The saint is in rapture as a teasing angel pierces her repeatedly with a golden arrow. Whatever she's up to, it's a stunning work. . . ."[1] Struck by this description, I consult another guidebook. It makes the same kind of remark, which essentially boils down to: "She looks pretty hot to me."

This annoys me. I bewail the spiritual illiteracy of a generation so unacquainted with prayer that they look into the face of a great mystic and see only nookie, as if Teresa were one of those ubiquitous, pouty-lipped teenaged models making a comic attempt to look sexy. Eventually, though, it dawns on me that this is a bit unreasonable, because Teresa's expression does indeed have a passionate cast. The guidebook authors are just creating a false contradiction between the mystical and the erotic, because of course much of mysticism is deeply grounded in Eros. Indeed, many writers have observed that the vocabulary of the spirit is of necessity the vocabulary of the erotic; as Dorothee Soelle has observed, "One cannot think of mystical experience and certainly not speak of it without eroticism."[2] At its deepest, you could say that prayer is a romance language.

You could say this, but if you do you're certain to offend people. Some traditions within Christianity are more in touch with this aspect of prayer than others. For those that aren't, it can seem alien and offensive, an inappropriate melding of spheres that should be kept discrete, like pedophilia, or having an affair with your shrink. The Franciscan writer and musician John Michael Talbot has faced this reaction:

> Many of my friends are shocked the first time they hear prayer being described in romantic terms. For them, there's something improper or even slightly sacrilegious about comparing prayer, a thing so lofty and spiritual, to love. But it didn't bother Francis or other saints. They could think of no better way to describe the union between God and humans.[3]

The problem with being scandalized by the use of romantic language in relation to prayer is that it ignores the existence of erotic mysticism from before the time of Christ and throughout the Church's history since, as well as the prayer traditions of other faiths. As Dorothee Soelle reminds us:

> Certain texts from the late Middle Ages manifest a playful language that delights in confusing eroticism and religion. . . . But these erotic wordplays have much older and deeper roots. Even if one reacts with mistrust or abhorrence to such mixing of eroticism and religion, one cannot deny the purely linguistic observation that repeated connections are made between mystical and sexual experience, and that it cannot be given expression without drawing on eroticism. The preferred place of mystical experience is eroticism.[4]

Rosemary Haughton affirms that "[t]he poetry of passionate love is the accurate language of theology."[5] Whether you read the Song of Songs as an allegory of the love between God and his people, or as a straightforward story of the passion between lovers that nonetheless made it into the Canon, there is no denying that God wants to say something to us here, and he's using a very sexual story to say it.

Long before Teresa picked up this theme in her *Meditations on the Song of Songs*, Bernard of Clairvaux, who evidently suffered no insecurities over his sexual orientation, seized on it: "I beg, I beseech, I implore: He should kiss me with the kiss of his mouth!"[6] Examples could be multiplied almost indefinitely— Dante Alighieri (a Tertiary), Lady Julian, Catherine of Siena, and John of the Cross are just a few. Francis, of course, was fluent in the romantic language of prayer: the *Absorbeat*, quoted earlier, is an example of his ardent longing for God. Francis also spoke of poverty—for him the highest of virtues—in romantic terms:

> He made himself poor because his beloved Christ had been poor. He espoused Poverty because she had been "the inseparable companion of the Most High Son Of God," and because for twelve centuries she has wandered about forsaken. In truth, it was a wonderful union. Never was a loved woman the object of a more chivalrous and loyal cult, of more impassioned and more charming homage. . . . "I pray you, point out to me," he said to two old men encountered in the country, "the dwelling place of Lady Poverty, for I faint with love for her."[7]

Indeed, Francis fell for Lady Poverty as hard as Dante fell for Beatrice, his lifelong obsession and the inspiration of his most sublime poetry. *The Legend of the Three Companions*, compiled by Francis' close friends Leo, Angelo and Rufino, tells how Francis first encountered Lady Poverty on a night of revels with his Assisian buddies before his life was transformed. His friends went ahead of him in the street singing, but Francis suddenly stopped, so absorbed in a surpassing sweetness that he later said he couldn't have moved if he'd been hacked into pieces on the spot. His friends finally turned around, and seeing him transfixed, started teasing him: "What were you thinking of? Why didn't you follow us? Were you thinking of getting married?" Francis responded, "You are right: I was thinking of wooing the noblest, richest, and most beautiful bride ever seen." This got exactly the kind of response you would expect, and the text continues: "The bride was none other than that form of true religion which he embraced; and which, above any other is noble, rich, and beautiful in its poverty."[8]

The second generation of Franciscans included mystics who picked up this thread and wove it into their own writings, Jacopone of Todi and Angela of Foligno being two notable examples. Here is Jacopone:

> Love, Love, You have wounded me,
>> Your name only can I invoke;
> Love, Love, I am one with You,
>> Let me embrace You alone.
> Love, Love, You have swept me up violently,
>> I want to faint, Love; may I always be close to You:
> Love, I beseech You, let me die of love.[9]

The writings of other mystics of the Middle Ages, especially women, are rife with romantic and erotic imagery: Marguerite Porète wrote of the *ravissant loin-près*, the enrapturing far-near One, God as the love who is at once unattainably distant and close enough to ravish. Mechtilde of Magdeburg wrote charming if rather daring dialogues between Lover and beloved, and others followed in the same vein. Some of these are identified in Wendy Wright's moving work *The Sacred Heart*, and she continues the tradition in her own poetry. Other recent examples include two I've cited already: the title of Rosemary Haughton's *The Passionate God* speaks for itself (as does Ronald Rollheiser's *The Holy Longing*[10]), and Dorothee Soelle's book *The Silent Cry: Mysticism and Resistance* devotes a chapter to the erotic as one of the principal "sites of mysticism."[11] Meanwhile Huston Smith lists it, along with asceticism, as one of the primary paths to God. Smith notes that there is a strong tradition of erotic mysticism within Islam as well, mainly identified with the Sufis, of whom the poet Rumi (a contemporary of Francis, whose spiritual style had much in common with his own) is perhaps the most famous spokesman.

The point is that this is an old path, trodden by some of the spiritual giants of the ages:

> Spiritual marriage, in which we relate to God as the lover of our soul, has been the foundation of Christian mysticism for centuries. Francis knew this kind of intimacy with God, although he wrote little about it. Other saints, like Teresa of Avila and John of the Cross, wrote extensive journals about their communion with God. . . .[12]

This path is not without its dangers; there have been cults in which the link between prayer and passion has been twisted to the point of blasphemy. But the authenticity of a thing isn't nullified by the existence of a counterfeit. Christ himself, in the Holy Eucharist, offers us intimacy with him through his flesh; as a friend remarked, "We are talking, after all, about eating someone's *body*." Throughout the history of the Church, there have been those who were scandalized by the Incarnation, and all that it implies: God taking human flesh, being subject to all its annoyances and temptations, even its destruction. As Rosemary Haughton says, "It violates, as a concept, our sense of divine and human decency, it crosses a barrier which we require, for our mental and psychological comfort, to be impermeable."[13] How messy this confusion of God and man, this melding of spheres that should be kept discrete. Why not be rid of the embarrassing doctrine, and declare that the Incarnation was an illusion, and that the spirit is good and the flesh an evil that must at all costs be kept from tainting the higher nature. The Church has fought this heresy vigorously, if not always charitably, as plenty of Albigensians would be glad to tell you if they'd been allowed to live. But the Church has never really rid itself of it—witness our preoccupation with the sins of the flesh, while we neglect "the weightier matters of the law, judgment, mercy, and faith" (Matt 23:23, KJV).[14]

Yet as much as we fear it, Eros is buried deep in our nature, in the nature of all creation, and even in the nature of God: as Dorothee Soelle reminds us, "Eros is one of God's names."[15]

Attraction is one of the fundamental facts of the universe: all creation is saturated with desire. Gravity pulls huge bodies in the heavens toward each other at unimaginable distances, and all matter is made up of unfathomably tiny particles, moving around each other in a perpetual dance. Life itself, recent advances in reproductive technology notwithstanding, is inseparably linked to desire, and much of human social life is organized around trying to contain, control and deal with the consequences of that desire which, because of our fallen nature, is frequently distorted into sin.

And God? What are we to make of a God who pre-exists all things, and yet is described as "love"? The doctrine of the Trinity resolves this paradox in a way that is notoriously difficult to articulate, but will be evident to anyone who's seen Rublev's famous icon, in which the three Persons are drawn together in an unending circle of desire. It's interesting that the icon represents the Three as angels of ambiguous gender. I understand why some people prefer not to use the masculine pronoun with reference to God, although I tend to do so because I don't want to be distracted by gender politics when I'm trying to pray. And yet, I love Rolheiser's description of the Trinity: "perfect masculinity and perfect femininity making perfect love." The point is that attraction and desire are deeply embedded in creation, and Eros is a fundamental force in human relationships, in the relationship between Persons of the Trinity, and in the relationship between humans and the God who draws them into relationship with himself by joining his body to theirs.

This is why the first and greatest commandment is to love God with *all* that we are: our heart, soul, mind and strength. As Francis put it in the *Rule of 1221*:

> With all our hearts and all our souls, all our minds and all our strength, all our power and all our understanding, with every faculty. . . and every effort, with every affection and all our emotions, with every wish and desire, we should love our Lord and God who has given and gives us everything, body and soul, and all our life. . . ."[16]

We love God most fully when all our passions are laid at his feet: our passion for social justice, for good workmanship, for learning; our passion for protecting and nurturing our children, and the passion that produced them. All are manifestations of a spiritual force that is ultimately meant to turn us toward God, the one who lit this flame within us before we were born. The reason Francis is still known, loved and followed by so many eight hundred years later is not his external virtues. Plenty of virtuous saints have been all but forgotten, and Francis would have been one of them had it not been for his passion.[17] But it would be a mistake to remove Francis from his context, and see his mysticism as one long sigh of uninterrupted bliss. In the tradition of courtly love, Francis knew passion in both its forms, both ecstasy and agony, the delight of God's presence and the anguish of his absence. He had enjoyed the divine embrace, but he also knew what it was to cry, "Why have You forsaken me?"

Recall Rosemary Haughton's description of the soul's longing for God: it can become overwhelming, exquisitely painful. Sometimes that desire feels like a bottomless well. But Christ himself sanctified our desire: "Blessed are those who hunger and thirst after righteousness"—including the righteous *One*, "the Lord our Righteousness" (Jer 23:6, KJV). Only an infinite God can satisfy a bottomless desire, and so our longing constantly directs us to him. As the thirteenth century holy women known as the Beguines[18] recognized, "it is precisely at that moment of agony of longing love that (wo)man is closest to God."[19] Mechtilde of Magdeburg, herself a Beguine, recorded a vision in which Christ instructed her to let go of everything else, including her hard-won "exterior" virtues: "It is only those that you carry within you by nature that you must desire to feel eternally: these virtues are your noble desire and your insatiable hunger which I shall satisfy eternally with My infinite superabundance."[20]

Well, so what? What's the significance of acknowledging the erotic underpinnings of mysticism; in short, now that I know that, what do I do? Acknowledging this is important because failing to do so blinds us to the very passion that was so powerful it erupted in the Incarnation; it gives us a truncated God. If we take them seriously, the words "God is love" convey something profound—indeed, something startling—about the nature of God. They're meant, in fact, to summarize that nature, as much as that's possible. We miss the significance of this altogether when we reduce the words to a trite bumper-sticker slogan, and our tendency to do this contributes to an impoverished view of God. An impoverished view is a distorted view—a false image, and we've been warned about that for a reason. We can't take our rightful place in relationship with God if we don't understand, at least to the extent humans are able, who God is and what he wants with us.

To apply erotic language to spiritual experience isn't dumping something sordid onto holy ground. Instead, it's taking seriously the Incarnational—*enfleshed*—nature of our faith, and the nature of Eros itself—that energy that runs like a single current through all the passions of which humans are capable. The creativity of the artist or the scientist, the pleasure and exuberance of an athlete's strength, the courage of a gifted statesman, the single-minded devotion of Francis—all these reflect the passion of humanity, which has its source in God. Yet although we pay lip service to the virtue of living life to the fullest, and celebrate from a distance those who seize the day and go for the gusto, at close hand that passion can be baffling:

> Francis appears unreasonable to those of us less smitten. He is a hero in love, his language and actions those of a person whose heart has been wounded by love, who is intoxicated by the perfume of the Beloved. To others the heroic lover always seems a bit mad, someone going through a phase, someone who will eventually pass from the insanity of *being in love* to the sanity and reasonableness of *love*. But that does not happen to Francis.[21]

Francis' love was extreme, and drove him to extreme demonstrations that sometimes embarrassed others and even himself.[22] The reason he didn't care is that when he looked at Christ, he saw something worth giving up everything for, including reasonableness and respectability.

In the movie *Jaws*, there's a great moment when Rod Steiger's character, the chief of police, has just caught his first view of the shark. His companions are happily gearing up for what they think will be a routine little shark hunt, when the chief turns to them with a stunned expression and says, "You're going to need a bigger boat." Those who have experienced the passion of God are wearing that same expression and saying to us, "You're going to need a bigger God—*much* bigger." We need to understand that the force with which God loves us broke through in the Incarnation, and in all the events that followed, because it's *big*—infinitely big. God became man because there is no "inappropriate melding of spheres that should be kept discrete." Eros runs from God's nature to ours and through the whole of creation. There is no keeping these spheres discrete, because there are no discrete spheres; as Teresa put it, "There is only *one* love." At the deepest level, God is the source and ultimate object of all our desire; this is why St. Augustine said that our hearts are perpetually restless until they rest in him. This restless longing, this chronic dissatisfaction, are actually signs of the mercy of God, who implanted within us a yearning that, though all our wanderings, constantly calls us home.

> Here then at home, by no more storms distrest,
> Folding laborious hands we sit, wings furled;
> Here in close perfume lies the rose-leaf curled,
> Here the sun stands and knows not east nor west,
> Here no tide runs; we have come, last and best,
> From the wide zone in dizzying circles hurled
> To that still centre where the spinning world
> Sleeps on its axis, to the heart of rest.
> —Dorothy L. Sayers, *Gaudy Night*[23]

Questions for Reflection

1. Do you find the use of romantic language and imagery helpful in expressing the soul's relationship to God? Why (not)? The Scriptures and other writings offer many other images: God as father or mother; Jesus as brother, friend, good shepherd. What kinds of imagery do you typically draw upon in your own prayer?

2. Have there been times in your life when you have felt a particularly strong longing or desire for God? What was going on at those times?

3. Is it news to you that God desires you? It took Teresa of Avila years to accept that she was *wanted* by God. Is this idea foreign to you?

4. Think back over your spiritual history. Can you identify times and ways in which it seemed God was pursuing you? Anne Lamott talks about being followed around by Jesus in the form of a black cat, who kept pestering her until she let him in. Have you ever had the feeling God was shadowing you?

Steps into Love

1. If the romantic/erotic language of mysticism is new or alien to you, it might help to become acquainted with its long history in the Christian faith. There are a number of excellent books on the subject, which could serve as a useful introduction. Try: *Passionate Spirituality* (Elizabeth A. Dreyer), *Brides in the Desert* (Saskia Murk-Jansen), *Sacred Heart* (Wendy Wright), *The Passionate God* (Rosemary Haughton), *The Holy Longing* (Ronald Rolheiser), *Women Mystics in Medieval Europe* (Emilie Zum Brunn and Georgette Epiney-Burgard), or *Visions and Longings* (Monica Furlong). *The Flowing Light of the Godhead*, by Mechtilde of Magdeburg, is one of the best examples of bridal mysticism from its high point in the medieval era.

2. Teresa of Avila struggled to believe that Christ wanted her. If you struggle with that too, spend some time looking at a crucifix. *That's* how much he wants you.

3. For Francis, it was the most natural thing in the world to be passionately in love with God, but for the rest of us, a love like that can seem completely out of reach. It's true that we can't conjure up love on our own, but we can ask for it. God in his mercy doesn't grant every silly request we make, but he's not likely to refuse this one. Ask.

4. Start by taking the steps you can. Spend time with him. Look at him. Dwell on his attributes. Think about how you've fallen in love with humans in your life; the process will be much the same.

Prayer

Lord, you have struck me with a wound to the heart, and nothing on earth could ever heal it. Nor could anything under heaven make me want it healed. Give me such a consuming love for you that, like Francis, I would be willing to suffer any ordeal and carry any cross for your sake. Amen.

5

PENITENCE
SHOW ME YOUR SCARS

Regular examination of our obedience to Christ is necessary. To be reconcilers we must first be deeply reconciled to God. We practice daily self-examination and regular use of the Sacrament of Reconciliation.

—*"What the Third Order Rule Is About"*[1]

MAYBE IT'S THE EX-NURSE IN ME, but I have an instinctive appreciation for sterility. There's something aesthetically pleasing about the idea of a sterile field: the complete absence of living organisms. There are so few moments of perfection in this world that a perfectly sterilized object seems a marvel, something truly admirable.

Of course a sterile field is, by definition, incapable of supporting life. If you want to cultivate the things that support life, you need a different kind of field, one with plenty of dirt. Manure also helps. The appeal of perfection probably explains the popularity of perfectly manicured lawns: seamless and unbroken, they cloak our suburbs in a mantle of green decorum. Yet what do people do when they really want to grow things— serious, life-sustaining things? They don't leave the ground perfectly clipped, velvety smooth like a golf course; instead, they go through and puncture it, stir it up, turn it over. It may be a systematic mess, but it *is* undoubtedly messy. And it's into the places that are broken open that they place the seed—the seed that will produce new life.

It's taken me a long time to appreciate this principle in the spiritual life. I'd read any number of people who emphasized God's ability to make use of our brokenness, to redeem our hurts and failures and use them to shape us into the people he always meant us to be. But until recently it remained a head-level thing for me, another of those things I hoped was true, but didn't *know* to be true, deep in my bones. It's Francis, and his followers in my time and place, who've helped me understand how life-giving that brokenness can be.

The Franciscan Third Order was originally known as the "Brothers and Sisters of Penance," which tells you something about Francis' priorities, and those of his followers. Francis' approach to penitence was exactly what you'd expect considering everything else we know about him: zealous, radical, single-minded and occasionally over-the-top, with just enough humor and joy to make him a saint and not a madman. Thomas of Celano, Francis' first biographer, tells us that Francis "never spared his body, but exposed it to every hurt both in deed and in word."[2] Building on Celano, Bonaventure later wrote that Francis

> mortified his lower appetites so strictly that he scarcely took enough food or drink to stay alive. . . . As long as he enjoyed good health, he scarcely ever ate cooked food. When he did, he mixed it with ashes or destroyed its taste, usually by adding water. He never drank enough water, even when he was burning with thirst—not to mention taking wine—and he devised ways of practicing even greater self-denial, becoming better at it day by day.[3]

Francis undoubtedly got better at it than any of us wants to be. Even granting Bonaventure a bit of pious exaggeration, it's true that Francis' austerities and privations took their toll on his health. At the end of his life he apologized to his body, which he affectionately knew as "Brother Ass," for having abused it.

But although Francis encouraged his brothers to join him in penances that would strike us as pretty extreme, he also made them lighten up from time to time. On one occasion, a brother cried out in the night from hunger, and Francis made everyone eat so the one friar would not be ashamed. At the famous "chapter of mats," where some five thousand friars gathered outside Assisi with only mats for beds, Francis was told that many of the friars were suffering greatly from the mail-shirts and iron rings they wore next to their skin. Many had fallen ill, some had died, and all were finding it mighty hard to pray in such extreme discomfort. On learning this, Francis commanded that everyone who had such items take them off and place them before him on the ground. A stack of more than five hundred shirts, and many more rings, formed a great heap in front of Francis, who ordered that they be left there.[4]

In his approach to penance, Francis was a product of his time, one that strikes most of us as excessive and unhealthy in its zeal to mortify the flesh. Yet in our time, first-world Christians at least may be equally unbalanced in our indulgence of the flesh, and I am as guilty of this as anyone. Where the balance lies is undoubtedly a fruitful subject for meditation, but there's another, healthier medieval practice that Francis was steeped in, and that was contemplating with sorrow the Passion of Christ. So great was his identification with the crucified Lord that toward the end of his life he prayed to be allowed two graces: to know the agony experienced by Christ in his crucifixion, and to know the love that compelled him to go through with it. About two years before his death, he spent forty days in seclusion at a cliff-side hermitage on Mount Alverna. On or about the feast of the Holy Cross (September 14), as he meditated on the Passion of Christ, he saw in a vision an angel who imprinted on Francis' own flesh the stigmata—the five wounds of the Passion.

It was the first known instance of stigmatization in history, and accounts for the centrality of suffering in the Franciscan spirituality that developed after the saint's death.[5] Francis bore these wounds for the rest of his life, keeping them covered as best he could—in Assisi you can see the slippers made for him so that he could walk with less discomfort, and the slip of fabric he used to cover the wound in his side. Devotion to the wounds of Christ grew in the centuries after Francis.[6] The thought of those wounds can reduce a person to a deep inner silence—the silence of genuine awe. But the significance of the wounds isn't just that they draw us to sorrow; they also bring us life, especially when we approach them with our own wounds. Jesus said (John 6:53–58) that it was by eating his flesh and drinking his blood that we would have life within us—the flesh broken open, the blood spilling from his wounds are the source of the life that sustains us. A life-saving blood transfusion requires that both donor and recipient be wounded; in the same way, I believe that the life we are promised flows most easily when it flows directly from Christ's open wounds to our own.

When we learn this lesson at a deeper level, it becomes possible not only to accept our own suffering, but to long for it. Calling suffering a "site of mysticism," Dorothee Soelle writes:

> Erotic mysticism and mysticism that is focused on the passion often flow one into the other, as in the infectious *Laude* of the spiritualist poet Jacopone of Todi (ca. 1236–1306): *Cristo amoroso, et eo voglio en croce nudato salire* (Christ, most beloved, I too will go naked onto the cross and there, in your embrace, die with you). For many pious mystics, it is more important to behold the man of sorrow and embrace the bloodied bridegroom than to meet the risen Savior. This longing finds its climax in stigmatization, the emergence of Christ's wounds on one's own body, as first attested to in Francis of Assisi.[7]

Later, Soelle finds a similar impulse in the work of the sixteenth-century mystic and poet John of the Cross, who:

> weaves into language what dolorous mysticism deeply yearned for, namely, stigmatization. Christ's wounds breaking forth in one's own body. Originally, the stigma was a wound, an injurious

stab wound inflicted on Greek and Roman slaves as a mark of identification, comparable to the numbers tattooed on the wrists and forearms of concentration camp inmates. In this sense the poetry of Saint John lives from an open wound.[8]

In some sense, I believe, we do too, and on the feast of the Stigmata of St. Francis (September 17) this hit me with real force. Short of drilling the holes myself, I'm not likely ever to bear the stigmata. But I realized that day that, like most people who've made it to middle age, I'm covered with wounds—many of my own making, through sin, and some inflicted by others. And each one represents an "entry port," where the life of Christ can penetrate.

What does all this have to do with penitence? Does it include suffering that results from our own sins? You could say that there are four types of suffering, at least, and I'll arrange them in descending order of spiritual impressiveness. There's suffering for the faith, or persecution. There's *compassio*, which Soelle defines as "suffering with Christ and all who suffer."[9] *Compassio* means allowing ourselves to feel the anguish of those whom this world grinds beneath its wheel, to resist the temptation to look away, and to force ourselves to absorb a little of the blow. There's suffering that comes from what the Augustinian prayer book calls "the contrariness of things," everything from the series of domestic mishaps that conspire to make us late for work, to the disease that strikes out of nowhere and brings life to a halt.

And then there's the suffering I bring on myself, by my own sins. These aren't the heroic wounds of martyrdom, or scars from courageously taking on the sufferings of others. They aren't even the inevitable bumps and bruises we all get from participating in the life of a fallen race. These are cowardly, self-inflicted wounds, the ones we acquired trying to flee whatever battle we were called to fight: the addictions we used to escape problems we were supposed to deal with, the lies and half-truths that left their mark on our conscience, the broken relationships that broke us a little as well. Our first impulse is to keep these wounds well bandaged and out of sight: we don't want to discuss them, see them, or think about them. But another thing I know from having been a nurse is that a lot of wounds heal best when exposed to air and light.

The Church knows this too, which is why it provides us with the tools for healing our wounds and being reconciled to God. Franciscan Tertiaries are no longer called "Brothers and Sisters of Penance," but penitence is still a core part of our Rule. We're expected to make a daily examination of conscience, and a daily confession of sin (the Daily Office includes this, and so does the Eucharist). We're also required at least twice a year to make sacramental confession—to confess our sins to God in the presence of a priest, who can offer the assurance of absolution. It seems to me that there are two types of believers: those who, like Francis, identify with St. Paul when he calls himself the "chief of sinners," and those who wonder what he was talking about. But both those who see themselves as sewers of iniquity and those who think they're pretty good people can be equally horrified at the thought of confessing their sins in front of another person. Roman Catholics have the edge here, because they get used to it at an early age. For Anglicans, the sacrament is offered but not required, and while I have no data to prove it, I'd bet that ninety-nine percent of Anglicans have never seriously considered it. Given that most Americans fear public speaking more than death, it seems likely that speaking—even to an audience of one—on the subject of one's sins isn't a prospect most of us would relish.

Which is a real pity, because the sacrament of reconciliation is such a gift. It's not about excoriating ourselves for our failures. Instead, the *Principles* describe it as the means "through which the burden of past sin and failure is lifted and peace and hope re: ored."[10] It is, just as the name implies, about reconciliation. The psalmist begs God, "Wash me thoroughly from mine iniquity, and cleanse me from my sin" (Psalm 51:2, KJV). There's nothing like the feeling of cleanness and restoration to wholeness that you experience after confession. Before entering formation in the Third Order, I had only made two confessions in my life, both in times of spiritual desperation. It was immensely helpful to bring my case before someone who could assure me of the forgiveness I'd been unable to find until then. Now that confession is part of my religious routine, it's sort of like getting a mammogram: not without its discomforts, but it's great to walk away knowing there's nothing deadly lurking in there. And one of the best things I've found in this discipline is how helpful it is to get some perspective on my faults from someone whose opinion carries authority. Being one of the "inner sewer" types myself, it's tremendously liberating to have someone hear the worst I have to offer and not actually collapse in horror.

Francis was also inclined to think the worst of himself, but unlike those of us who just choose to live with the neurosis, he had the courage to confront his shadow side and be reconciled to himself, and to God. One of the most famous stories told about Francis concerns the time when the people of the town of Gubbio were being terrorized by a bloodthirsty wolf. The wolf had killed several people, and the townsfolk were afraid to leave their homes. So Francis decided to go meet the wolf; his companions accompanied him part of the way, but finally out of fear left Francis to confront the beast alone. When he found the wolf, it lunged at him open-jawed, but when Francis greeted it as "Brother Wolf" and commanded it not to harm him or anyone else, it stopped and knelt in submission at Francis' feet. Francis and the wolf made a deal: the people of the town would provide food for the wolf for the rest of its life, in exchange for the wolf's ceasing to harm them. The wolf bowed its head and placed its right paw into Francis' hand, and sealed the deal. So the wolf lived in peace with the people of Gubbio for the rest of its life.[11]

This is actually true. Well, it might be. The reason this story has such a central place in Franciscan lore is that it points to Francis' role as a reconciler of enemies. But a deeper reading suggests that Francis was unafraid to go forth alone and confront the beast within himself. This is a very Franciscan approach to penitence: Francis didn't *kill* the wolf—he *tamed* it so that he could live with it in peace. Likewise, our wounds—even the scary, shameful, self-inflicted ones—shouldn't become occasions for doing ourselves further violence. They're to be occasions of mercy, of reconciliation, of peace. Can we accept this? Can we see our wounds as places where the divine life can enter into us? Would so great a king be willing to enter through such humble doors?

Yes, absolutely—provided that they are *humble* doors, and not *closed* doors. When we come to grief over our sins, both in the sense of ending in failure and ending in mourning, they can be an effective way of bringing down our defenses against God. We can bar the doors to God by insisting that we're beyond forgiveness, and some of us do that. But surely one of the more impenetrable defenses we raise against God is the belief that we're good people who don't need him. Not only are we usually wrong about how "good" we are, but this attitude so completely misses the point. No other parents would be satisfied with raising children who lived "good" lives but never wanted anything to do with them. Why should God be content with children who are upstanding and respectable but alienated and estranged from him? So anything that brings down the illusion of our self-sufficiency can cause our defenses to crumble, and bring us, between mouthfuls of dust, to admit our need for God. And perhaps a mouth that is open in confession is yet another entry port through which God's life can break through to us.

Questions for Reflection

1. While the Roman Catholic Church requires periodic sacramental confession of all its members, the Anglican approach has been characterized as, "All may, none must, some should." What kinds of criteria would you use to determine whether to confess privately to God, or to make use of the sacrament of reconciliation? Would it depend on the seriousness of the sin itself, or perhaps on your inability to accept God's forgiveness and move on? Some other factors?

2. Have you had the experience of making a confession before another person, whether a priest, pastor, or lay person?

What was the experience like? How did you feel before your confession? Afterward?

3. What criteria do you use to take stock of your life: a formal method of self-examination, an informal attentiveness to the stirrings of conscience, something else? How often do you do this?

4. Some people tend to gloss over their faults, while others are prey to self-condemnation. Which direction do you lean: would you say that your tendency is to be too easy on yourself, or too hard? Does your answer suggest a change in the method or frequency of self-examination you practice?

Steps into Penitence

1. The Scriptures are full of references to penitence, and meditating on these is a good place to begin. Psalm 51 is a particularly moving expression of remorse and a plea for forgiveness: "Have mercy upon me, O God, according to thy lovingkindness: according unto the multitude of thy tender mercies blot out my transgressions" (Psalm 51:1, KJV). The Bible also encourages us to make auricular confession: "confess your sins to one another, and pray for one another, so that you may be healed" (James 5:16).

2. Experiment with making self-examen, or the examination of conscience, a regular part of your spiritual life. Many people find it helpful to review the day just before bedtime. For those of us who don't do our best thinking—or indeed, any thinking—at night, morning may be a better time.

3. There are several methods of examen. A simple one I use is to go over the past day, looking for signs of God's grace as well as the occasions where I fell short. You might like to organize it around the two great commandments, and ask yourself what things in your day brought you closer to love of God and neighbor, and what things got in the way. Don't forget that your "neighbor" includes the poor of the world who are out of sight, and frequently out of mind. If you have a personal Rule of life,

that is, if you've chosen a set of spiritual practices to serve as the structure of your spiritual life, your examen might consist of a review of your Rule with an eye to which parts are drawing you closer to God and which need some attention. Each of these methods can be used as a quick daily examen; with more time and deeper attention, they can also be used for a more comprehensive examination of conscience such as you might perform during penitential seasons (Advent and Lent), or before making your sacramental confession.

4. You might like to use a formal prayer of confession after your daily examen. The one I use most days comes from the Book of Common Prayer:

Most merciful God,
we confess that we have sinned against you
in thought, word, and deed,
by what we have done,
and by what we have left undone.
We have not loved you with our whole heart;
we have not loved our neighbors as ourselves.
We are truly sorry and we humbly repent.
For the sake of your Son Jesus Christ,
have mercy on us and forgive us;
that we may delight in your will,
and walk in your ways,
to the glory of your Name. Amen.

5. If there is a sin that is troubling your conscience—perhaps a particularly serious sin, or just one that has tripped you up over and over—consider confessing it to God in the presence of another person. Depending on your faith tradition, this person might be a priest or minister, a spiritual mentor or trusted friend.

6. Even if there is no particular burden on your conscience, you might want to experiment with making sacramental confession during the penitential seasons of the year. It's not a bad idea to clean up a bit before greeting the infant Jesus or the risen Christ.

Prayer

Lord, there are times when I would give anything to be clean. Not even sterilized—I would settle for clean. Just to be presentable enough to be in your presence would be worth whatever it took. Sometimes it feels like I'm covered with nasty wounds. Francis washed the wounds of lepers, and it seems you are willing to wash mine. Give me the humility to accept your cleansing touch, and when you have forgiven me, give me the grace to forgive myself. Amen.

BROTHER BIRD
THE MYSTERY IN THE GARDEN

Most High, omnipotent good Lord, to you be praise, glory,
   honor, and all blessing.
Only to you, Most High, do they belong and no one is worthy
   to call upon your name.
May you be praised, my Lord, with all your creatures. . . .
                              —Francis of Assisi, *Canticle of Brother Sun*

THERE'S A MYSTERY BIRD in our garden. My husband and I are in
Cambridge for his sabbatical, and the college where he is a visiting
fellow has assigned us to a very nice two-bedroom flat on the second floor of a three-flat house. The décor has a kind of Franciscan
feel, which is to say that it isn't fancy, though it is spacious and
comfortable. It looks out over a nice garden, with bright green
lawn, flowering fruit trees, weeping willow, and daffodils rashly
announcing the arrival of spring. It's quiet and peaceful here,
about a mile out of the city center, beyond the "Backs." But
there's a mystery bird in our garden, and it keeps itself well hidden
while making the most appalling noise.

   At first we weren't quite sure what we were hearing. We both
had the flu when we got here, complete with fever and chills, and
in our delirium we each privately thought we were imagining it.
Besides, we were honking like a pair of Canada geese ourselves, so

it was a little hard to sort out the bird's sounds from our own. But once the fog began to lift, we recovered enough presence of mind to consult each other, and determined that this was no hallucination. Out of the lovely blend of birdsong that issued from the normal creatures flying about in the vicinity, there was no denying the presence of the mystery bird, but we were at a loss to explain its call, or even to describe it. It's a kind of squawking sound, sort of like a chicken only louder and more obnoxious, and it only does it once or, if it's really worked up, twice. This happens about every two to three hours, and there seems to be no answering call from a second bird. I pointed out that this was no surprise: what kind of creature would mate with something that sounded like that? I decided it most resembled a driver grinding the gears of a very small car. The persistent "*Fawk! Fawk!*" suggested a rude and rather limited vocabulary, but then I've known people like that.

The mystery bird became a frequent topic of our conversations, a source of entertainment in a place where there are only four television channels and we haven't paid the TV tax, so technically it's all illegal anyway. My husband would come home to my reports on the mystery bird's activity that day: "The bird was really excited today—I heard it every twenty minutes or so." We speculated about what original sin the species had committed to be cursed with the ugliest song in all of birddom, deciding that it must have eaten the forbidden seed. The thing that was most intriguing about it, though, was that we never actually saw it. I would hear it grind its gears, and I'd go rushing to the window, and there would be nothing there. And then it would be mute again for another few hours. Coming home by the footpath that leads past our hedges, I would peer in, but could never find it. I once passed the college and saw a man throwing breadcrumbs through a railing, and though I had heard the telltale cry, I still couldn't see a bird there. Maybe it was a kind of local mania, a collective hallucination, and we'd already succumbed?

I was becoming obsessed. One day when the bird was especially lively, emitting a spirited "*Fawk!*" about every ten to fifteen minutes, I grabbed the end of a loaf of bread, and started throwing bits of it out the window toward the hedge. I wondered what the charming Chinese couple downstairs thought of the sudden storm of bread raining down outside their window; probably just another variant of the unfathomable Cambridge weather. The bird kept up its squawking, but didn't deign to appear, and the bread was consumed *in toto* by a passing squirrel. At one point I'd just about talked myself into a bird that looked like a crow with a neon orange beak, but it really didn't seem plausible that a sound like that could come from something so small. Later my husband came home, and I was idly gazing out the bathroom window (which perversely has the best view in the house), confessing my failure to elicit the bird, when I saw it. "Hurry—come quick, the bird is out!"

It was *huge*. Sort of rust colored, with a bright red face, green neck, and long trailing tail feathers. Not being a "birder" under normal circumstances, I wouldn't swear to that description in court, but it was huge. My husband joined me at the window and decided it was a pheasant, pointing out that it would be much nicer—and much quieter—on a plate. I said that if pheasants sounded like that, it was no wonder people wanted to shoot them.

Which made me think of Francis. Francis is of course famous as a lover of animals, and especially for preaching to the birds when the humans wouldn't listen. Many Franciscans nurse a mild resentment at the way Francis has been reduced to a figure on a birdbath: domesticated, separated from his radical message and rendered utterly unchallenging. I think one of the reasons Francis begged people not to canonize him in his lifetime was that he understood how much easier it is to dismiss people once they become saints. Saints are by definition different from the rest of us, or so we tend to believe. And once they become that different, we no longer have to take their message or their example personally, as something meant for ordinary mortals like us. Safely trapped in stained glass, or consigned to the birdbath, they also can no longer follow us when we choose to walk away.

Meanwhile, there's a bird swearing violently in our garden. I think it's quite possible that if Francis were confronted with the mystery bird, he would be less inclined to invite it for a gentle bath than to turn a squirt gun on it, but maybe that's just me. Because the truth is that Francis, like Christ and like the mystery bird, said things I don't want to hear. And there are two predictable human reactions to those who tell us things we don't want to hear: we either trivialize them or we kill them. It's either the birdbath or the cross. Not a bad thing to remember, because if we're faithful to our own calling, then our voices will be no more welcome: "Remember the word that I said to you, 'Servants are not greater than their master.' If they persecuted me, they will persecute you; if they kept my word, they will keep yours also" (John 15:20). And if they have dismissed me as quaintly irrelevant, don't think it can't happen to you.

6

HUMILITY
BEYOND DEGRADATION
AND SELF-ESTEEM

Tertiaries always keep before them the example of Christ, who emptied himself, taking the form of a servant, and who, on the last night of his life, humbly washed his disciples' feet. They likewise seek to serve one another with humility.

Humility confesses that we have nothing that we have not received and admits the fact of our insufficiency and our dependence upon God. . . .

The faults Tertiaries see in others are the subject of prayer rather than of criticism. They take care to cast out the beam from their own eye before offering to remove the speck from another's. They are ready to accept the lowest place when asked and to volunteer to take it. Nevertheless, when asked to undertake work of which they feel unworthy or incapable they do not shrink from it on the grounds of humility, but confidently attempt it through the power that is made perfect in weakness.

—*The Principles of the Third Order of the Society of Saint Francis*, Days Twenty-Two to Twenty-Four

THERE'S A DEEP AMBIVALENCE ABOUT HUMILITY in the Western Church these days. We seem split between two conflicting mindsets, suspended between our heritage and our culture. The former points us to our fallenness, our capacity for evil, and our need for redemption. The latter tells us, "I'm okay; you're okay." Not being brilliant or beautiful, rich or famous, I know that the world beyond my own circle of family and friends has very little use for me, and even less for those who are struggling on society's margins. Yet a label inside one of my jackets bears the assurance:

I am unfettered
Unbound
Triumphant
Glorious and
Splendid

It doesn't add, "I am sounding somewhat defensive and more than a little ridiculous," but it should. The Third Order Rule calls us to humility; can Francis help us steer a course between a sense of worthlessness and the goofy affirmations alternately offered us by the culture in which we live?

Thousands of years of our spiritual ancestry invite us to contemplate our unworthiness before God. The psalmist cries, "Have mercy upon me, O God, according to thy lovingkindness: according unto the multitude of thy tender mercies blot out my transgressions" (Ps. 51:1, KJV). Jesus speaks approvingly of the tax collector, who "would not lift up so much as his eyes unto heaven, but smote upon his breast, saying, God be merciful to me a sinner" (Luke 18:13, KJV). St. Paul, calling himself "wretched" and "the chief of sinners," complained that he could not seem to do the good he wished, but kept doing the evil he wished to avoid (Romans 7:19).

St. Francis was very much at home with this attitude. Brother Leo, one of Francis' earliest followers and dearest friends, once overheard him in prayer, saying, "My God and my all, who are you, my sweetest Lord and God; and who am I, a poor little worm, your servant?"[1] This was no pious posturing—after all, he had thought himself alone with God. It was how the great saint really saw himself: poor, small, a "worm," a slave. And he took care to remind himself of this at every opportunity. On one occasion, Francis made a series of self-accusations, and ordered Brother Leo to confirm each time that he was worthy of hell. Leo strove to obey, but was unable to say anything but that Francis was blessed by God and certainly bound for heaven.[2] Another time, when Francis was preaching in Terni, the bishop rose up and gave thanks that God had chosen to illuminate his Church "through this poor, undistinguished and unlearned man Francis." Francis fell at the bishop's feet and thanked him for describing him this way, when others were too apt to call him holy.[3] He liked to caution those people not to be in such a hurry to canonize him, as his battle with the flesh was not yet won: "I can still have sons and daughters."[4]

But Francis wasn't only meek before his social equals and superiors. Once as he passed through the field of a peasant, the man ran up to him and begged him to live up to his reputation: "Try to be as good as you are said to be by all men," the peasant begged, "for many put their trust in you." Francis fell down and kissed the man's feet, and thanked him for the admonition.[5] But Francis' humility reached further down the social scale even than that. Once when he felt he'd been unwelcoming to a leper and hurt his feelings, he did penance by sitting down with the leper to a meal:

> [A] bowl was put between them. Now the leper was completely covered with sores and ulcers. His fingers, which he used to eat with, were eaten away and tinged with blood, so much so that when he put them into the bowl, blood dripped from them.[6]

Nor was Francis a stranger to the lash: once when he was tempted by what Thomas of Celano delicately calls "the enticement of the flesh," he scourged himself till he was covered in welts, then threw himself naked into the snow. He accompanied this treatment with a lecture to "Brother Ass," his body, on how richly the punishment was deserved. The means Francis used to cultivate the virtue of humility ranged from the charming to the disturbing; there's a reason the word "Gothic" has taken on the connotations it has. Francis was indeed a product of his time, and in this regard at least, his time was one of extremes. The penances and mortifications of the flesh that devout men and women practiced in the Middle Ages are responsible for all the darkness, pathology, and excess conjured up by the term "medieval."

We don't really go in for that sort of thing anymore. Instruments for inflicting pain on oneself still have a market among the sexual fringes, but religious people mostly leave them alone. But we've also abandoned figurative self-flagellation along with the literal: who now wants to pray the old confession, in which we called ourselves "miserable offenders," and declared that the memory of our sins "is grievous unto us; the burden of them is intolerable"? In a culture that worships self-esteem, those who describe themselves in Francis' terms are likely to end up on Prozac, and perhaps some of this is a healthy corrective to the wallowing "worm theology"[7] of the past. But has our understanding of humility improved, or are we just experiencing another mindless arc of the pendulum, exchanging the blind spots and prejudices of the Middles Ages for those of our own age?

The Church hasn't entirely forgotten about humility, of course. We do sometimes speak of "brokenness," of the ways God strips us of our false supports, our ego, so that we become empty and impoverished before him. It's not that uncommon to come across preachers and writers who deal beautifully with the subject of how God's strength is made perfect in our weakness, our brokenness, and our poverty. And as long as it all remains at a fairly abstract level, most Christians nod in assent.

Yet when it threatens to become more concrete, I often detect a sudden change in the atmosphere. The moment someone expresses a lack of self-confidence or a sense of personal unworthiness, weakness or failure, others rush in to correct the situation. Those at risk of humility are told they have "low self-esteem," and that their negativity is actually false humility. They're admonished not to be morbid, morose, or, worst of all, "medieval." Francis, after all, could be lauded for being careful to preserve a low opinion of himself and appear worthless in the eyes of others. . . . He used often to remark, "What a man is before God, that he is and no more." Consequently he was convinced that it was foolish to be elated when people showed him marks of respect; he was upset by praise, but overjoyed when he was insulted. He liked to have people scorn him—that spurred him on to do better—and hated to be praised, which could lead to a fall.[8]

Eight hundred years later, things have changed. Any hint that we're feeling less than admirable is apt to be met with a reminder that Jesus said we must love our neighbor "as ourselves," so clearly we're meant to love ourselves. True enough, except that by "loving ourselves" people often seem to mean we should *like* ourselves, accept ourselves, and think of ourselves as pretty decent people. Certainly we are meant to respect ourselves at some level—after all, we're God's creatures, made in his image, however distorted the current reflection might be. But when do we join our voices to that of the psalmist, and cry to God "out of the depths"? And where is the writer in our day capable of lines like these:

There is no soundness in my flesh because of thine anger; neither is there any rest in my bones because of my sin. For mine iniquities are gone over mine head: as an heavy burden they are too heavy for me. My wounds stink and are corrupt because of my foolishness. I am troubled; I am bowed down greatly; I go mourning all the day long. (Ps. 38:3–6, KJV)

Express these sentiments in your Sunday morning church class, and I guarantee that no one will sit next to you ever again.

So we're left with the reality that while we bear the divine image, we have distorted that image, at times beyond recognition. What response to this constitutes true humility? Maybe this sounds like a silly dilemma, or a false one. And maybe the fact that I've been truly mystified by it says something rather humbling about my own intellect. But I've been on the receiving end of the "low self-esteem" speech and found it baffling. In his infinite generosity God has allowed me enough weakness, inadequacy and failure in my life to ensure that, if I'm not exactly humble, at least there are certain illusions of strength and self-sufficiency that I can't seriously entertain. But each time I looked to the Scriptures or the likes of Francis for hope that my screw-ups might be redeemed by bringing me closer to humility, I came up against this modern notion that it's more important to be "healthy." I believe the Church needs to be true to its countercultural calling, and call pride and vanity by their true names, instead of gutlessly assimilating into secular culture and worshipping at the shrine of self-esteem. And yet I know that a model of humans as morally bankrupt and degraded is not the last word in humility. How might this dilemma be resolved?

We could begin by returning to Francis' own prayer: *My God and My All, who are you, my sweetest Lord and God; and who am I, a poor little worm, your servant?* Francis may be "a poor little worm," but he doesn't begin there. He begins with "My God and my all," "my sweetest Lord and God." One thing I've come to understand about humility is that I can *be* sinful, empty, broken and bankrupt, but it doesn't matter nearly as much as I thought. The majesty and sweetness, the beauty and glory of Christ obliterates all of that. All that I most feared about my fallen nature may be true, but in the presence of God, somehow it's no longer important—or even relevant. The three disciples who witnessed the transfiguration of Christ were terrified, sensing that they were a bit out of their league. Peter, as usual, started babbling. But then the cloud overshadowed them, and their fears and limitations became unimportant next to the overwhelming fact of Jesus' glory. So do mine. When I realize this, it takes the focus off of me, and puts it on God, where it belongs. When I can see myself realistically, and then forget what I have seen because I am looking at God, then I am beginning to learn humility. And when I am realistic about my spiritual condition, but not obsessively interested in it, then I am drawing closer to genuine humility.[9]

And then Francis continues: "Who am I . . . *your servant?*" In spite of his poverty, he assumes his rightful, joyful place in the Lord's service. Francis had once aspired to be a knight in the service of a great worldly lord—until God pointed out that he would be better off following the Master than the servant. For Francis, to be the servant of Christ was an exalted position that implied privilege and conferred glory. The second thing I've learned about humility is that belonging to Christ means sharing in his glory. So when Christ embraces us, he isn't "stooping down" to some degrading level; he isn't slumming. He made us to be creatures who would *belong* in his embrace ("in your infinite love you made us for yourself. . . ."[10]). And in taking away both sin and the effects of sin, he's restoring us to what he always meant us to be—to our "rightful" and exalted place. He's not transforming us into something other than ourselves, but making us *completely* ourselves.

When I see it this way, I see myself very differently: I have indeed screwed up everything that was in my power to screw up, and left to my own devices, would be utterly lost. But at the same time, I was created to be something magnificent, and when Christ's work in me is complete, that's exactly what I will be. I don't find it so difficult to respect this creature, my true self. Unlike the "bankrupt and degraded" model, this view doesn't leave us in our wretchedness, burrowing through the earth like worms. But unlike the "healthy self-esteem" model, it doesn't resort to facile reassurances that deny our fallen nature. And once we have a truthful view of ourselves, we can also have a realistic understanding of the role we're meant to play in the world,[11] neither over- nor underestimating the scale of the impact we're called to have. As Francis put it, a picture of Christ painted on wood gives glory to Christ. The wood and the paint don't attract attention to themselves, or try to steal the glory; they do their job unnoticed. Francis is often referred to as the *poverello*, the "little poor man," and a large part of his greatness lay in his willingness to be small. Once I give up my image of myself as either gold or sawdust, I can get on with being a serviceable block of wood, and there's real freedom in that. Francis knew that all along, of course. How else could he see humility as the road to perfect joy?

Questions for Reflection

1. How do we steer a course between the twin evils of destructive self-loathing and vacuous self-esteem? Imagine that you're in a relationship with someone who's unreasonably demanding and selfish. When is it best to respond with gentleness and acceptance, and when is it right to assert yourself? How would you know?

2. Jesus gave his disciples a powerful example of humility by washing their feet, a thing not even slaves could be made to do unless they were foreigners. But how do we follow this example, given that foot washing is not a meaningful gesture in our culture? Whose feet are we to wash in our time and place, and how?

3. The *Principles* remind us of Jesus' teaching that when we're in company, we shouldn't pursue the place of honor, but seek the lowest place. What are some social settings in which status-seeking takes place? How could a person "seek the lowest place" in those settings? What spiritual benefit is possible from doing this?

4. What about status-seeking in our consumption? We are constantly being urged to buy products on the promise that they confer prestige on those who possess them. What about the things you own? Which did you buy for purely functional reasons, which for their inherent beauty or other qualities, and which represent bids for status?

Steps into Humility

1. The next time you're at a party, reception or other social occasion, scan the room for the person with the lowest status, who may seem nervous, shy or intimidated. Try befriending that person. Then reflect on how others respond to your hanging out with someone like that.

2. If you're in a leadership position (administrator, boss, teacher, officer), think about what it would mean to serve the people

under you, as Jesus did. Find ways to wash their feet by putting your own interests aside and meeting their needs. Parents, unless you're actually neglecting or abusing your children, you're already doing this, so relax. But perhaps thinking of your role in this way can help you do it with greater joy.

3. The next time you find yourself being driven crazy by the faults or annoying habits of those around you, take a moment to reflect on your own. It's a crowded planet, and existence today means we all need a lot of patience with each other.

4. Try an experiment in status reversal. The next time a waiter, sales clerk or other person in service is unhelpful or rude to you, stop yourself before insisting on what you're entitled to. Imagine that person is your superior—your boss, your parent, a member of the clergy or a respected public official—and respond accordingly. How does that change the content and tone of your answer?

5. Humility isn't a virtue we can gain by focusing closely on it, because there's no way to decide you've got it without losing it. If you worry about this, you can quickly find yourself in a hall of mirrors where you decide you're not humble so that you can be, but then you're aware of it so you're not. The best advice I've heard on this comes from Richard Foster, who has written extensively on the classical spiritual disciplines and virtues, including the virtue of humility. Foster counsels anyone caught in this trap to have a good laugh at himself and forget about it.[12]

6. A better way to cultivate humility is to pray for it. Ask God to help you see clearly the truth about yourself—or at least, as much truth as you can handle. Then see what happens.

Prayer

Oh God, I know what I've done with my life, and what I deserve. But I also know that the treatment I deserve was never your intention for me. And I know that your Spirit is at work within me, transforming me into someone who would dazzle me if I could see her now. Just help me to cooperate, would you? Thanks. Amen.

7

SELF-DENIAL
LIFE WITHOUT ANESTHESIA

Jesus calls those who would serve him to follow his example and choose for themselves the same path of renunciation and sacrifice. To those who hear and obey he promises union with God.

—The Principles of the Third Order of the Society of Saint Francis, Day Three

[Self-denial] is the discipline of saying "No" to oneself by putting God first. We are often aware of the places in our lives where additional self-discipline is needed, but our Spiritual Directors should be asked to help in this area. We also focus on eliminating the ways we may manipulate others to our own ends.

—"What the Third Order Rule Is About"

KATHLEEN NORRIS HAS SAID THAT THE SAINTS are those who have been willing to go through life without anesthesia.[1] We humans are natural anesthesiologists, in the same way that we are born idolaters: we are constantly looking for alternatives to God for relief from pain, for reassurance, security and pleasure. The ways we devise to dull our suffering are almost infinitely varied: some resort to illicit drugs while others prefer caffeine, cigarettes or chocolate. Some people take refuge in work, while others find it in play: sports, television, shopping or sex. In short, the means of dulling our pain are as diverse as the pains themselves: tension and pressure, loneliness and boredom, disappointment and loss are all scary signs of our raw, wounded humanity, and all good reasons to don the anesthesiologist's mask and take a deep breath.

Certainly Francis was willing to do without anesthesia. One of the more famous stories told about Francis concerns the Lent he spent on an uninhabited island in a lake near Perugia. He was staying with a friend who lived nearby, and he asked his friend to row him out to the little island on the night of Ash Wednesday, so that no one would know where he'd gone. He took with him two loaves of bread, and asked the man not to return for him until Maundy Thursday. When he returned for Francis, he discovered there was still a loaf and a half left; apparently, Francis knew that Christ had fasted a full forty days, and he'd eaten half a loaf to avoid the sin of pride. *The Little Flowers*[2] records that God performed many miracles on that island after Francis' solitary Lent, so that soon people began to settle there. I've visited this island; there's not much going on there even now except for a couple cafés and a few ladies who sit in the sun and do needlework. But it does seem a holy place, and without a doubt Francis had very little recourse to anesthesia during his sojourn there.

With Norris' observation and Francis' example in mind, I decided that my Lenten discipline one year would be to try to make it through Lent without anesthesia. The first thing that happened was that I failed. The second thing that happened was that a friend asked me, "What's so bad about anesthesia? Why give up things that make life more pleasant, or even bearable? Is there something inherently positive about pain?" But although the idea of de-anaesthetizing myself resonated deep within, I couldn't articulate the reasons why. I stammered unintelligibly for a bit, and then promised to get back to her. I managed to stall until Holy Week, when I really had to figure out what I thought I'd been doing for the past six weeks.

It's easy enough to see the point of self-denial if it leads directly to someone else's benefit: for example, if I fast and donate the money I would have spent on the meal to a food bank. The point of other forms of self-denial is a little harder to fathom, though—one thinks of hair shirts, and fanatics spending their lives sitting on poles for the glory of God. These days we tend to think that, while God can use suffering to make us stronger, we shouldn't seek it out deliberately; life itself can be relied upon to provide all the pain we need. Is the decision to forgo anesthesia a step back from this healthy change in our thinking? Is it just the pointless pursuit of pain for its own sake, and is there in fact something inherently positive about pain?

Well, yes—sometimes. As an ex-nurse, I know that there's a time to relieve pain, and a time to wait and see what it has to tell us. One of the things that made leprosy[3] such a fearful disease was that the loss of sensation allowed people to sustain hideous injuries without realizing it. The function of pain is to signal that something is wrong with us, and we won't get this message if we're numb and nodding off. Likewise, a state of mindless inattention can cause us to miss messages about things that are wrong with other people: we cannot be fully present to them, and awake to their problems, when we're caught up in our own little buzz. An extreme example of this is people who entertain company with the television on; "background music" is a less extreme point on the same continuum, and a standing point of contention in my household. I figure if the music is good, it deserves my full attention; if not, it deserves to be turned off, and the company deserves my full focus. I don't see myself ever winning this argument.

A weakness of mine is mindlessly turning on the radio when I'm alone, at home or in the car. It's a popular one, I suppose. I'm not sure why we do it, but I know it's a bad sign. The seventeenth century philosopher Blaise Pascal said that ninety percent of the problems of humankind stem from our inability to sit quietly in a room by ourselves. We'll do almost anything to avoid it, and the walkman, iPod and cell phone now guarantee that we can drag our anesthesia with us when we go outdoors, like a bag on an IV pole, so that even nature gets half our attention. In Aldous Huxley's vision of the future, unlike Orwell's, people would not be kept in submission through force; instead we would end up "amusing ourselves to death."[4] Seduction, not rape, would be the preferred method; subjected to an endless stream of entertaining trivialities, we would eventually have neither the capacity nor the will to think about anything important, including our own situation.

Without putting it in such conspiratorial terms, I do think this is a trap many of us find ourselves in. The constant barrage of entertaining trivialities issuing from the mass media is itself enough to keep us from thinking of anything scary, like the meaning of life, for example, or the fact that we are dust, and to dust we shall return—maybe before the day is out. With the September 11 terrorist attacks, a lot of people spoke of waking up to the fact that life offers no guarantees, and they vowed not to continue taking their lives and loved ones for granted. But why were they asleep in the first place? People die suddenly every day; why did it take planes flying into buildings to realize that the spouse they fought with this morning might not come home tonight? The mid-life crisis, so rich in comic potential, is a more common tragedy: we wake up at age forty or fifty to realize that life is passing us by, and all is vanity. Perhaps if we'd sat quietly in a room by ourselves at age thirty, without anesthesia and without distractions, we might have seen this coming, and not gone to sleep in the first place. The thirteenth century Sufi poet Rumi also wondered why people were so habitually inattentive, and so slow to grasp the richness of life: "Why, when God's world is so big/Did you fall asleep in a prison/of all places?"[5] Perhaps if we'd silenced the static long enough to hear the still, small voice, God himself might have warned us. But the meaning of life and the fact of our mortality, along with a lot of other things God might want to talk to us about, are far too frightening to be faced if we can avoid them. So we count backwards from a hundred, and let ourselves drift off.

I'm not saying that every time I turn on the radio I'm fleeing the prospect of personal annihilation; sometimes I just want to hear the news. And it's not that the things we use for anesthesia are necessarily bad in themselves, although some are. Cigarettes are unhealthy, shopping puts you in debt, and chocolate—well, as someone said of beer, chocolate is a sign that God loves us and wants us to be happy. But the choice of anesthetic is a very personal one, and one person's mind-numbing escapism is another's harmless pleasure. I don't need to be a teetotaler, because I'm not tempted to abuse alcohol; it's those who habitually use it to self-medicate who probably should consider giving it up. A greater temptation for me is to use credentials to relieve my sense of insignificance in the world. Honorifics like "Doctor," the initials "PhD" after my name, and an impressive institutional affiliation, can become anesthesia by conferring a sense of importance, and it's easy to be lured into this trap when you have them.

Francis wasn't keen on titles or prestigious forms of address. He named his band of followers the "Order of Friars Minor," which doesn't say much to us now, but it said a lot then. In Francis' time, as in ours, people were striving for upward mobility, fighting their way up the ladder planted on the backs of Europe's serfs, with rungs ascending through the peasantry, the emerging middle class, and the nobility. The common people were known as *minores*, the nobility as *majores*; Francis' father was one of those who succeeded in rising from the former to the latter. But Francis had no time for such status-striving. By calling his brothers Friars Minor, he indicated that they were to be "little brothers."[6] He emphasized this to a bishop who asked him once if his friars would not make good candidates for certain church offices:

> Lord, my brothers are called minors so that they will not presume to become greater. Their vocation teaches them to remain in a lowly station and to follow the footsteps of the humble Christ, so that in the end they may be exalted. . . . I pray you, therefore, Father, that you by no means permit them to rise to any prelacy, lest they become prouder rather than poorer and grow arrogant toward the rest.[7]

Inevitably there was a need for people to hold positions of leadership in the Order, but Francis was attentive to the same principles in naming them. He called them "ministers" at a time when that title wasn't common, making the point that their leadership was to be characterized above all by service.

The temptation to use offices or titles to wrest a little deference out of others is seductive. When I deny myself the exploitation of this or any other privilege (such as being white or middle class), it forces me to deal with others from a position of greater equality. Without this anesthetic, I can awaken to my own need for recognition, and be alert enough to remember that my true worth comes from God.[8]

Of course, most people don't have the luxury of worrying that the world will confer excessive status upon them. Yet there's a closely related temptation to which nearly all of us yield at times, and it also concerns speech—specifically, the ways we speak about ourselves. Much of our speech consists of what sociologist Erving Goffman[9] referred to as "self-presentation," the dramatic enactment of ourselves so that our audience sees the mask we've chosen and not the face beneath. We're constantly explaining, justifying and staging ourselves to mold others' perception of us into that which best serves our ego. As Richard Foster has said,

> The tongue is our most powerful weapon of manipulation. A frantic stream of words flows from us because we are in a constant process of adjusting our public image. We fear so deeply what we think other people see in us, so we talk in order to straighten out their understanding. If I have done some wrong thing and discover that you know about it I will be very tempted to help you understand my action![10]

We humans are so very skilled in the subtly manipulative uses of language. Justification, flattery, half-truths and diversions, code words and jargon are all tools we use to position ourselves to advantage.[11] Spending a few days listening attentively to our own speech can rouse us to some pretty uncomfortable truths, and point us toward another powerful form of self-denial, namely, honesty and humility in our speech.

Manipulative communication isn't just practiced by individuals, however. In our politics and our culture, propaganda and stereotyping are potent anesthetics that dull our capacity to see others, especially enemies, as human beings. One of the many ways Francis practiced self-denial was by denying himself the luxury of enmity. In the earliest days of his movement, he and his first companions took shelter in a little hut by a brook called Rivotorto. They lived there at least a year in the most primitive conditions, when one day a peasant marched in and claimed it for his donkey. Francis offered no resistance, but graciously moved his brothers on to another place.[12] On another occasion, three notorious robbers came to a hermitage where Francis and some brothers were staying, while Francis was out begging for bread and wine. Brother Angelo sent them away with a sermon on the evils of stealing, especially from the servants of God. When Francis returned, however, he gave Angelo a sermon of his own. He then ordered Angelo to find the robbers and offer them the bread and wine, and beg their forgiveness for his lack of charity. Angelo obeyed, and the robbers were converted by the love they were shown. When they returned to the hermitage, Francis welcomed them "with kindness and holy affection."[13]

Francis' commitment to reconciliation wouldn't let him demonize others, even when those others presented a real threat. How comforting it is to let the real human beings on the other side of our wars disappear into a blur of dehumanizing stereotypes. How much easier it is to kill them, or to support others' killing them in our name, if we don't have to see them as real people. Likewise, how reassuring it is to think that those who suffer want while we enjoy plenty aren't really like us, so they probably don't even know what they're missing. The thought of a global system that offers us "low, low prices!" through the under- or uncompensated labor of the most vulnerable people on the planet is painful enough to make us reach for anything that will make them less real. Francis didn't allow himself this luxury, because he saw the "Other" as not only human, but divine; that is, he looked at them and saw Christ.

We all need anesthesia at times, and when we do, the proverbial stiff shot of brandy can be a real gift. There are times when a full dose of reality could be lethal: the fact that we typically respond to tragic news with shock and disbelief is undoubtedly a blessing, and a kind of natural anesthesia. It buys us a bit of time, and allows us to take the truth in gradually so that we're not crushed by it. But when we use anesthetics in an ongoing, habitual way, they can become dangerous. It's one thing to take pills for an occasional pain, but taking them every day for years on end without pausing to turn our attention to the source of the problem is definitely unwise. And that's just it: anesthesia keeps us inattentive. A chronic state of half-witted numbness isn't the best place from which to hear God's voice and discern the truth about our lives.

The self-denial part of the Franciscan Rule allows a lot of scope for individual experimentation and creativity, as people try to root out the places in their lives where they need this kind of discipline. I can't imagine that there are two Tertiaries whose practices of self-denial are identical, and that's as it should be. But I would bet that most forms of self-denial could be seen as a way of agreeing to go through life—at least, part of life—without anesthesia. This, too, is as it should be, because while we don't actively seek out pain, in consenting to feel such pain as life brings us, we're following our Master's example. Jesus was offered anesthesia on the cross, but he refused it: "They offered him wine mixed with myrrh; but he did not take it" (Mark 15:23). The gospel doesn't tell us why, but I assume he wanted to be fully awake to what was going on—to live the experience of saving humankind, not sleep through it. At the beginning of his ministry, Jesus had resisted the temptation to win people over with spectacular displays of power, choosing instead to do the tedious, messy and sometimes painful work of changing people's understanding of God one by one. At the end of his life, he remained true to this commitment: presence, not escapism, agony rather than numbness.[14] This is the way of the cross, the way Jesus invites us to follow, and if we can just keep our eyes open, we'll see it for what it is: the way that leads to life.

Questions for Reflection

1. What are some forms of anesthesia that might not be immediately obvious? One thing many of us do to feel better in the context of an argument is to insist on having the last word. What others can you think of?

2. Where is the line between unhealthy self-indulgence and legitimate celebration? Drowning our sorrows can be self-destructive, yet Jesus' first miracle was making wine for a party. How do you know the difference?

3. Our choices for anesthesia are influenced by our family and cultural patterns, as well as our individual tastes and temperaments. Think about the forms you use, whether alcohol, food, drugs, work, shopping, television or whatever you reach for to dull your pain. What messages have you received about these things from your family? What messages do you receive from the culture—through advertising, peer influences, mass media or elsewhere?

4. What are some ways you can resist these messages? What counter-messages does your faith offer?

5. Societies, like individuals, can search for ways to dull pain. Dehumanizing the enemy during wartime is one example; filling the news with fluff and omitting coverage of suffering around the world is another. In what ways do you see our society seeking escape from things that might be painful to face?

Steps into Self-denial

1. Make a list of your favorite forms of anesthesia, your "drugs of choice." Think about how, when and why you use them.

2. For each of the major forms you use, ask yourself: How does it affect others in your life? Does it make you less available to them now, or threaten to take you from them in the future? Do they worry that your behavior is unhealthy or self-destructive?

3. Experiment with going for short periods without one form of anesthesia you typically turn to. It's probably not realistic to go

cold turkey on all of them forever, so start small. Try turning off the television for a week; you might keep a journal of how this feels, and what you learn from it. When the time is up, how does it feel to turn it on again? Consider increasing the amount of time you go without: perhaps this would make a good plan for Lent?

4. Try practicing self-denial for a cause. One example popular with young people is the "thirty hour famine," which you can learn about at http://www.30hourfamine.org. Or you might give up going out for lunch or seeing a movie once a week and donate the savings to a food bank or other worthy cause.

5. If you have a seriously unhealthy or even life-threatening addiction, seek help. There are numerous recovery groups such as Alcoholics Anonymous, as well as smoking cessation programs, and support groups for just about anything that might be ruining your life. Your doctor or clergy member can help you find the help you need. However much you may loathe yourself, know that God does not share this opinion. He loves you and wants you to be free, so let him help you.

Prayer

Lord, you said that if we want to come after you, we must deny ourselves, take up our cross, and follow you. We don't really want to do this. But we *want* to want to, at least sometimes. We ask you to supply what is lacking in our loyalty. Give us a love great enough to follow you to the cross, and the grace and courage to endure every pain and grief we meet on the way—including the pain of those most unlike ourselves. Amen.

8

SIMPLICITY
AFFLICTING THE COMFORTABLE

Tertiaries, though they possess property and earn money to support themselves and their families, show themselves true followers of Christ and of Saint Francis by their readiness to live simply and to share with others. They recognize that some of their members may be called to a literal following of Saint Francis in a life of extreme simplicity. All, however, accept that they avoid luxury and waste, and regard their possessions as being held in trust for God. Personal spending is limited to what is necessary for the health and well-being of themselves and of their dependents. They aim to stay free from all attachment to wealth, keeping themselves constantly aware of the poverty of the world and its claim on them. . . .

> —*The Principles of the Third Order of the Society of Saint Francis,* Days Eleven and Twelve

SIMPLICITY IS THE MOST CHALLENGING PART of the Rule for me. I've been to the townships of South Africa and the "high density areas," as they are euphemistically called, in urban Zimbabwe. I've visited the shelters where AIDS orphans are housed, and the hospices where the more fortunate of their parents have died. I've seen the mud-and-manure huts where the rural people of Botswana scratch out an existence. I've also seen the dwellings of the *campesinos* of Colombia, and the makeshift shelters they erect when they come to the city and its promise of employment goes unfulfilled. I've seen the maimed adults and hungry children begging on the cathedral steps in Bogotà, and the men and women sitting idle on their front steps in the inner-city neighborhoods of de-industrialized Pittsburgh, where work has long disappeared, and hope with it. So I guess I'm "aware of the poverty of the world," and have a deep if rather vague sense that it has some kind of "claim" on me. What I don't know is what exactly that claim consists of, or what to do about it.

I know what Francis did about it: he became one of them. He espoused himself to Lady Poverty, and spent his whole life singing her praises and seeking new avenues of downward mobility. He took Jesus literally when he said, "If you wish to be perfect, go, sell your possesions and give the money to the poor, and you will have treasure in heaven; then come, follow me" (Matt 19:21). In his biography of Francis, Thomas of Celano comments that Francis "was rich in having only a tunic, a cord, and drawers, and he had nothing else. His poor habit showed where he was laying up his riches."[1] Francis gave away everything he had to the poor, not just once at his conversion, but throughout his life. Once when Francis was returning to Assisi from Siena, he and his companion came across a poor man on the road. Francis said to the other brother, "We must return this mantle to that poor man to whom it belongs. We borrowed it from him until we should meet someone poorer than ourselves." The other friar refused, concerned that Francis would ruin his health by neglecting himself to provide for others—which he in fact did. But Francis insisted, saying that to keep something when another's need is greater than our own constitutes theft.[2]

On another occasion, when Francis and Masseo were making a road trip to France, they split up in a village to beg something to eat. Francis was kind of a puny guy and not terribly attractive, so didn't fare as well as Masseo, who was tall and handsome. When Masseo turned up with a bag full of the evidence of his popularity, Francis rejoiced that he could add vanity to the list of things he had to do without. So when they sat down to a picnic on the bare ground, Francis kept repeating, "Oh Brother Masseo, we do not deserve such a great treasure as this!" Masseo, pointing out that they had neither a tablecloth nor a table, no dish, knife, bowl, waiter or house, asked what exactly Francis had in mind when he spoke of "treasure." Francis replied that their meal was a treasure because it had been supplied entirely by divine providence.[3]

I have begged a meal or two in my time, but it's been a while. Frankly, when I read these stories about Francis, his way of living seems so far from mine that it's hard to imagine in what sense my life could ever be considered "Franciscan." As academics, my husband and I are not among the more highly paid professionals, but our combined incomes put us easily into the top five percent nationally. We live in a house that is comfortable, beautiful and absurdly large for two people; it is also too large for us to maintain ourselves, so we pay other people to maintain it. I even pay someone to walk my dog on my longer workdays, a thing that makes my mother roar with laughter, although, as I like to point out, she never hesitated to hire nannies for us when she was otherwise occupied. Moreover, I drive a car that was bought new and is still new enough to be reliable; I have a weakness for sushi, espresso and other expensive treats; and although I don't buy jewelry for myself, I do have enough of a collection to decorate a moderate sized Christmas tree. I'm not terribly extravagant in my clothes, but that's partly because I despise shopping. It's interesting to consider what Francis stipulated as an appropriate wardrobe for a female Tertiary:

> The sisters in turn shall wear an outer garment and tunic made of cloth of the same price [as the men's] and humble quality; or at least they are to have with the outer garment a white or black underwrap or petticoat, or an ample linen gown without gathers, the price of an ell of which is not to exceed twelve Pisa denars. . . . They are not to wear silken or dyed veils and ribbons.[4]

I suppose it would be rather unseemly for Francis to be so well acquainted with ladies' underclothes, had his family not been in the clothing business. It's a little difficult to translate this into a useful set of guidelines for a twenty-first century university faculty member, but the salient point is clear enough: I have more money than I need, and spend a good bit of it on myself. As a result, giving away ten percent of my income doesn't exactly cut to the bone, and even if it did, my husband makes roughly twice what I do, and I still have the full benefit of *his* income. So the question I wrestle with—which all the more comfortable bits of Christ's body must deal with at some level—is this: how can I reconcile my standard of living with the call of Christ, and the needs of the poor? As a Franciscan, my specific challenge is to make my life consistent with the example of Francis, and the *Principles of the Third Order.*

Simple, you think: move into a smaller house on a bus line, sell one of the cars, sell the jewelry, live on half your family income and give away the other half. There's a catch, though: being married means that I don't make these decisions unilaterally. My husband grew up in real poverty and is incredibly generous with what he now has. If he's unapologetic about what he has left, I can understand that. An anti-materialist stance may be the luxury of those born to comfort; perhaps Francis himself wouldn't have been so quick to renounce worldly goods had he not had the opportunity to exhaust their charms early on. But of course, he did renounce them, quite dramatically:

> Tired of military adventurism, the young Francis began to divest himself of his considerable material possessions, thereby incurring his father's displeasure. A life-changing break with Don Pietro came in front of Assisi's good bishop when Francis literally removed the clothes given him by his father and uttered the startling statement: "From now on, I can walk naked before the Lord, no longer saying 'my father, Pietro Bernardone,' but 'Our Father who art in Heaven.'"[5]

81

Like Francis, I too renounced material possessions at a young age, though unlike Francis, I got to keep my clothes on. At seventeen, I left my parents, gave up such possessions as I had, and joined a group of radical Christians who subsisted on donations in order to spend their time serving God and the poor. At this point, however, my story departs rather sharply from that of Francis. For one thing, Francis was to the end of his life a faithful son of the Church, always accountable to spiritual and ecclesiastical authority, whereas the group I joined tended not to bother about such things, and as a result, got a lot of things spectacularly wrong. More immediately, however, I discovered that my joining the ranks of the poor didn't help them very much. I could assure myself that I was free of the taint of worldly goods, but I seemed to spend all my time asking others to support me—mainly the poor themselves, since they were always more generous than the rich. But most importantly, perhaps, as an uneducated, unskilled teenager I had nothing much to offer "the poor," and so the whole thing was rather pointless, little more than a grand gesture that was more about my self-image than anything or anyone else— sincerely as I meant it at the time.

Now, having compromised my early ideals, I am less easy in my conscience, but probably better placed to make some sort of contribution. In my sociology courses, I regularly teach students about global inequality and the consequences of our official and individual decisions for the lives of people in developing countries. I also teach them something about racial and class inequalities within our own country, and push them to question the comforting assumption of equal opportunity that is part of our national mythology. This is prophetic work; as Kathleen Norris says, "A prophet's task is to reveal the fault lines hidden beneath the comfortable surface of the worlds we invent for ourselves, the national myths as well as the little lies and delusions of control and security that get us through the day."[6] Beyond this, I do the occasional homeless feed, and a bit of work for an organization responding to the AIDS crisis in Africa. And like most busy professionals, I write a few checks and hope they make a difference.

Still, I wonder about the poverty of the world and its claim on me. If you consider the top half dozen most easily and cheaply prevented diseases around the world, which are also the most easily and cheaply treated, together they kill over 35,000 children a *day*.[7] That's over ten times the total killed in the September 11 attacks, every day, every year. Every two days, these diseases kill more children globally than the total number of Americans who died in the Vietnam War in over ten years of fighting.[8] And that's not counting those who die of starvation. Each one of these children bears the image of God, and each one is as precious to its parents as ours are to us.

> Then he will say to those at his left hand, "You that are accursed, depart from me into the eternal fire prepared for the devil and his angels; for I was hungry and you gave me no food, I was thirsty and you gave me nothing to drink, I was a stranger and you did not welcome me, naked and you did not give me clothing, sick and in prison and you did not visit me" . . . "Truly I tell you, just as you did not do it to one of the least of these, you did not do it to me" (Matt 25:41–43, 45).

The poor of developing countries surely are some of the least of Jesus' brethren, and he assures us that whatever we do for them—or fail to do—he will take personally. *That* is poverty's claim on us: the God we claim to honor, whose name we bear, is wasting away in a Harare slum, or watching her child die of malaria or starvation, or sitting discouraged on a Pittsburgh stoop. Do we recognize him? The reason Francis is more than a figure on a birdbath is because, as Bonaventure put it, he "saw Christ's image in every poor person he met and he was prepared to give them everything he had, even if he himself had urgent need of it."[9] When a poor man asked alms of a friar at an awkward moment and the friar brushed him off, Francis made the brother strip off his habit, throw himself at the beggar's feet and ask his forgiveness, reminding him, "My dear brother, when you see a beggar, you are looking at an image of our Lord. . . ."[10]

To recognize the divine image in the poor has radical implications, and this is why, if we're paying attention, Francis poses such a challenge to us. When we avoid eye contact with a panhandler, or skip over the news accounts of famine in Africa, or fail to respond to natural disasters beyond our borders, Francis is saying to us: "What's the matter, Christians—don't you recognize your own God?" To say that the poverty of the world has a "claim" on me is to say that I owe something to the poor, that it is, in fact, theft if I keep it. But what is the nature of that debt? And given what I learned the last time I gave up my possessions for the sake of the poor, what can I do that might be more than an empty gesture—particularly when, as a married person, I cannot force my conclusions and commitments onto my spouse?

There are models. When my research took me to Budapest, I stopped at the Basilica of St. Stephen and sat for a while before the statue of St. Elizabeth of Hungary (1207–1231), a Tertiary and one of the patrons of the Third Order. Her arranged marriage to Ludwig IV, Landgrave of Thuringia became, against the odds, a love match, and her husband deeply respected her spiritual commitments, though he did not necessarily share them. These "commitments" increasingly placed her at odds with the court of Thuringia, as Elizabeth lost faith in the complacent notion that earthly inequalities were ordained by God. The young princess "began to experience the needs of the poor as a shameful judgment on her own luxurious lifestyle. She was stunned to realize that she was living on what had been taken away from others."[11] Others have arrived at this consciousness before and since, of course. What intrigues me about Elizabeth is how, from her privileged position, she responded to it with authenticity and grace.

She didn't nag or harass her husband, or try to guilt him into changing his lifestyle for her. Instead, she regulated her own consumption, and left his to his conscience. She dressed simply, gave extravagantly, and cared personally for the poorest lepers and beggars. She annoyed her mother-in-law by refusing to wear her crown in church, and scandalized her own maids, whom she joined in the household chores, by asking them to call her by her first name. The most touching example in my view, however, is the "food prohibition" she undertook on the advice of her confessor (who was, incidentally, one of history's great control freaks, but he did have a good idea now and then). She made it her business to know which food on the table came from her husband's own property, and which came from the extorted contributions of the poor, and she limited her own consumption to the former. She made no show of this—she pushed the illicit food about on her plate to give the appearance of eating it—nor did she expect anyone else to follow her in this practice. But Elizabeth was constantly aware of the poverty of the world and its claim on her. The key to her awareness lay in recognizing Christ himself in the face of the poor:

> On the way to Eisenach, in the middle of a frightful storm, she is supposed to have seen a child in rags on a woodpile, looking at her with great, disappointed, old man's eyes. "Where is your mother, child?" Elizabeth asked. The legend goes on to report that where the woodpile had been, a cross shot up, on which hung the dying Christ. He looked at her, and his eyes were the eyes of a child.[12]

Elizabeth was left a widow at the age of twenty, and without Ludwig's protection, was frozen out of the castle at Wartburg. This freed her to embrace a still more radical lifestyle, which she did with such gusto that she was dead at twenty-seven. But I learn less from the radical poverty of her widowhood than I learn from the simplicity of her life in the castle. When Elizabeth embraced poverty she suffered much discomfort, but at least she had settled the issue. Simplicity, by contrast, requires eternal vigilance, because the option to indulge oneself is never completely closed off. Which is the greater challenge is debatable, but for those of us trying to practice simplicity, the question is always before us: "How much is too much?"

I don't have a definitive answer to this question; simplicity is a moving target, and resists definitive answers and reassuring legalisms. What I do have is the example of King David: when God instructed David to make an offering on the threshingfloor of Araunah the Jebusite, Araunah offered David animals from his own herds for the holocaust. But David insisted on paying for them, saying, in effect, *I will not offer to the Lord my God that which has cost me nothing* (2 Sam 24:24). I don't know how much is enough, and how much is too much, but I do know that if our offerings don't cost us something, if we aren't giving until we really feel it, we're probably not giving enough. If our giving doesn't change our lifestyle, if it doesn't cut into our comforts somehow, that probably suggests something to us about the depth of our love, both for God and our neighbor. For most of us, simplicity regarding material possessions is ultimately a process. If we're not in a position to embrace complete poverty, or if that isn't God's call to us, we'll have to keep examining our lives for things we can change to live more fully into this ideal. But when love for God and neighbor come first, the question is never, "How much do I get to keep?" but "What else can I give?"

Maybe it would be easier to relinquish our hold on our possessions if we considered the extent to which they burden us. A number of writers have commented on the degree to which the things we own impose on us, requiring that we store them, dust and polish them, insure, alarm, guard and repair them. Francis understood this. When a bishop remarked to him that it seemed very hard to have no possessions at all, Francis replied, "My Lord, if we had any possessions we should also be forced to have arms to protect them, since possessions are a cause of disputes and strife."[13] Brother Leo once had a vision in which a group of friars with burdens on their backs were trying to cross a river, but fell in and were swept away by the current. Then other friars came without any loads and passed safely over the river. When Leo told Francis about the vision, the saint took it as a warning that possessions can weigh us down to the point of endangering our spiritual survival. Eight hundred years later, we need this warning more than ever.

Before leaving this subject, I want to bring up a form of simplicity that would actually require most of us to take more, and give less: that is, simplicity in our use of time. We live in a society where the pace of life is constantly being increased; it's like being trapped in some demented video game. If you're lucky enough to have a job at all, you're probably overworked and chronically short of time, distracted and exhausted. Those who are raising kids are definitely overworked and short of time, even those who don't do paid work on top of it. Even the kids are overworked, shuttled from one activity to the next when the school day is done. At a playing field near my house, which I can see from my study window, there are soccer games going on practically non-stop, including late at night and early weekend mornings. Even my retired parents complain of not having enough time. My friend who's in *prison* complains of not having enough time. Why do we live like this?

We can blame ourselves for some of it. We take on activities that we don't care about or aren't called to, either because we don't know how to say no or we just don't pause to examine whether they fit into our priorities. In our day, the unexamined life isn't worth living because it's too *exhausting*. A friend reported that he came home one night in the middle of Advent to find his wife collapsed on the couch with a migraine, the result of too much pressure to attend too many holiday functions. No wonder many people dread that time of year; in what way does anxiety and exhaustion turn us toward the coming of Christ—unless we're praying to be "raptured" before the next party? But all year long we're tied to our cell phones so that, as the ads enthusiastically tell us, we're never out of reach. For some people—brain surgeons, maybe, and real estate agents—being in touch is crucial. But for the rest of us? Even a fetus is only tied to one other person, which strikes me as an excellent plan. The only person who currently has my cell phone number is my husband. My own parents don't have my number, nor does my sister, because they live far away so they don't need to call and find out why I'm late. To be available at all times to anyone who might like to call is to me a vision of hell. I have the option to say no to this, just as I can say no to serving on another parish committee, attending parties given by people I don't know or like, or subscribing to magazines I'm never going to read.

On the job, though, we have less control. The struggle to free up time in my own life has shown me how hard a task this is, how necessary it is, and how very Franciscan it is. My solution was to forego the major reward of the academy—tenure—and take a position as a senior lecturer. This position also carries less prestige and a lower pay scale, but because I'm evaluated only on my teaching, it frees me from the crushing pressures of "publish-or-perish" and allows me a life outside my office. Because I'm in a high ranking department, I know a lot of famous scholars, and they all have the rewards that go with fame: job security, raises and the respect of their peers. I also know that these rewards no longer interest me, because they say nothing of importance about the quality of my life: "to be laid in the balance, they are altogether lighter than vanity" (Psalm 62:9, KJV). Discovering that I no longer cared about these things was a hugely liberating point in my Franciscan journey. Francis understood, and I'm coming to understand too, that the less we "need" things, the less they can control us.

The radical sociologist C. Wright Mills said, "Nowadays men often feel that their private lives are a series of traps."[14] What I learned from my job change is that often there is a way out of the trap we find ourselves in, a way toward a simpler and more satisfying existence, but it may involve relinquishing things that we assume are non-negotiable. Liberation for me has been a great joy, but it also means the daily acceptance of second-class citizenship in the academy. The notion that we can have it all and do it all is another of the "lies and delusions" we live with, one of the great seductive ideas of our time. And it leads us straight into workaholism, one of the great idolatries of our time. We slave away for this false god, when the real one has the compassion to *order* us to take a day off each week. Violations of the Ten Commandments don't get much attention in these days, yet some of these violations—say, adultery, or murder—we at least have the decency to be ashamed of. Others, such as the profaning of God's name, are just dismissed as irrelevant. The commandment to observe a day of rest is the only one whose violation we have made into a positive virtue, rewarding those who are "dedicated" to their jobs as if dedication itself were praiseworthy, and it doesn't matter what we're dedicated *to*.

What's the remedy? How do we untangle ourselves from the sticky web of demands spun around us by our jobs, society's expectations, and even our volunteer commitments, family responsibilities, and other worthy claims on our time? The Quaker writer Thomas Kelly observed that we feel stretched to the breaking point because our lives are ruled by committee:

> The outer distractions of our interests reflect an inner lack of integration of our own lives. We are trying to be several selves at once, without all our selves being organized by a single, mastering Life within us. Each of us tends to be, not a single self, but a whole committee of selves. There is the civic self, the parental self, the financial self, the religious self, the society self, the professional self, the literary self. And each of our selves is in turn a rank individualist, not co-operative but shouting out his vote loudly for himself when the voting time comes. . . . We are not integrated. We are distraught. We feel honestly the pull of many obligations and try to fulfill them all.[15]

The answer, Kelly says, is to dissolve the committee and replace it with a monarch—a view that was as countercultural in his time as it is in ours. The spiritual life is rife with paradoxes, and one of the great ones is that liberation comes through obedience. As Sören Kierkegaard put it, "purity of heart is to will *one* thing," that is, the absolute sovereignty of God. When we silence the whining voices of our committee, and are attentive to the one voice at what Kelly called the "divine Center," we find that we no longer spend all our time judging between competing claims, and feeling a sense of unmet obligation to whichever ones lost the last round. Only one voice matters, and when we have heard and obeyed it, we can be at rest.

What simplicity ultimately comes down to is attentiveness: only by paying attention to that voice at the Center can we hope to distinguish between what's truly important in our lives, and what is distracting us away from the truly important. If it's material consumption we're concerned with, we need to be attentive to the distinction between necessity and luxury, to the suffering of those who go without, and to the subtle but undeniable connection between our consumption patterns and theirs. When our use of time is the issue, a continual attentiveness to the divine prompting at the Center can give us the freedom to say no, even to very worthy claims on our time, in security and peace. And when the time comes to say yes, we can do so with courage, knowing that if we're truly following the divine will, we'll be given what we need to see it through.

Questions for Reflection

1. Imagine you've just died, and you're waiting to be ushered across the threshold. With you are a number of other people in the same condition, all of them from the poorest parts of the world. They've known hunger, lost children to malnutrition and disease, watched family and friends die of AIDS, been unjustly imprisoned and tortured for speaking the truth. What changes would you need to make in your life right now to be able to look each of those people in the eye and say, "I did everything I could"?

2. In what sense, if any, do you believe the poverty of the world has a "claim" on you?

3. Which would you find more challenging, voluntary poverty or simplicity? Why? Which of these comes closer to your sense of God's call to you? How do you interpret Christ's invitation to sell all, give to the poor, and follow him? Is it possible to have material possessions without being unduly attached to them?

4. If you live with others, how can you balance your desire for simplicity with their needs and priorities?

5. What criteria would you use to distinguish between the possessions and time commitments you should keep in your life, and those you should relinquish?

Steps into Simplicity

1. Take a mental inventory of your possessions. Then consider your time commitments. In each category, are there some things that are more trouble than they're worth? What might you do about them?

2. Consider the next level of objects and commitments: of some value, but not really necessary. Can you do without these? Keep moving inward until you arrive at the things that you strongly believe are worth keeping.

3. Go over your categories again, bearing in mind Francis' statement that to keep something when another person has greater need of it is theft. Is your house a cache of stolen goods? Want to reconsider which things are worth keeping?

4. One way to check our attachment to our possessions is by singling out an object we particularly value, and giving it away.[16] Is this experience—or the thought of it—wrenching or joyful? Painful or liberating?

5. The next time someone asks you to take on some commitment, don't give an immediate answer. Try telling the person you're being careful about not taking on more than you can realistically do, and promise to respond shortly. Pray about it, think about it, and if you don't feel led to do it, say "No." And try not to apologize—though that may be the hardest part.

6. There are a number of excellent books on simplicity, offering both analyses of why we might want to simplify our lives, and practical advice on how to do so. Some of my favorites include: Richard Foster, *Celebration of Discipline* and *Freedom of Simplicity*; Robert J. Wicks, *Everyday Simplicity: A Practical Guide to Spiritual Growth*; Delia Halverson, *Living Simply, Simply Living*; Andrea Van Steenhouse, *A Woman's Guide to a Simpler Life*;

Tracey McBride, *Frugal Luxuries,* and *Simplify Your Life, Living the Simple Life* and *Inner Simplicity* by Elaine St. James. There are lots of others, as well as newsletters, websites and other resources. But beware of those who simply use the buzzword "simplicity" to sell you more junk, with the promise that it will free up all your time and make you spiritual in ten easy steps.

Prayer

Oh God, when I compare my life to that of Francis, I feel like I've fallen facedown in the mud. Even if I had the radical commitment he had, I'm not exactly sure how I'd go about living it out in my time and place. Show me one thing I can do today to come a little closer to Francis' example. Help me to take that step, not out of guilt, legalism or shame, but out of love. Amen.

GHANA
RADICAL OPENNESS
AND REDEMPTION

Both here and in all your churches throughout the whole world,
we adore you, O Christ, and we bless you, because by your holy
Cross you have redeemed the world.

—Prayer attributed to St. Francis

Won't you help to sing
These songs of freedom?
'Cause all I ever have:
Redemption songs.

—Bob Marley, "Redemption Song"

MY MENTOR IN GRADUATE SCHOOL, trying to interest me in
tourism research, pointed out that people who study tourism get
to do their field work in some of the most pleasant places in the
world. This is generally true, and it's been my privilege to spend a
good bit of time in Wales studying nationalism and national iden-
tity, and the ways these are represented and even constructed in
museums and other heritage attractions. Yet for some perverse
reason, I've lately taken an interest in "atrocity tourism," that is,
museums that tell stories of extreme injustice. Now my fieldwork
is taking me to sites that focus on the Holocaust, apartheid, the

civil rights struggle, state terror under Communism, and geno-cide. The settings are pleasant enough, but the stories these muse-ums tell concern some of the most obscene outrages that human beings have perpetrated against one another, exposing our fallen nature at its depths. It's the side of us that didn't stop at killing God himself, and like the crucifixion narratives, the stories told at atrocity museums raise uncomfortable questions about which part we might have played ourselves, had we been there.

There's no shortage of material for this research; were it not for the limits of time, money and emotional endurance, one could go on collecting atrocity stories indefinitely, circling the globe. But there *are* limits, so I must content myself with a few examples that vary by atrocity type, time period and region. I can't see this project being complete without a section on the Atlantic slave trade, however, and this is what brought me to Ghana. There are a string of castles and forts along what used to be called the "Slave Coast," built by Europeans to protect all kinds of trading includ-ing, eventually, trade in human beings. The first of these was Elmina, built by the Portuguese in 1482; along with the nearby Cape Coast Castle, it is extremely well preserved and serves as a principal site for the interpretation of the history of slavery for vis-itors from Ghana, elsewhere in Africa and around the world. Many African Americans and others of the "diaspora" come here to see the places where their ancestors were taken away in chains. Para-doxically, it's a kind of pilgrimage site: one of the unholiest places on earth. And although Ghana is politically stable and economi-cally well off compared to many of its neighbors, it's still a poor country whose population struggles to get by. As such, Ghana would raise in new and urgent ways the issues surrounding the "simplicity" part of the Rule, reminding me again of the poor of the world and their claim on us.

My plane touched down in Accra, and I walked into a wall of heat and humidity. Living in the Northwest, I'm unaccustomed to heat and had already started thinking of Ghana as "Sauna." My hair is a natural humidity gauge: sticky conditions make it grow bigger and bigger, till by the end of a day in Miami I look like a country music singer. In Accra, by the time I cleared immigration, retrieved my bag and reached my hotel, it had frizzed itself into a horizontal position, where it would have remained for the duration but for the discipline of the French braid. At last I checked into my four-star hotel, chosen because it offers out-of-town taxi service, saving me from having to sort through the confusion of buses, bush taxis and tro-tros that might or might not get me to Elmina and back. Okay, I'll admit that I also chose this hotel because I was nervous and looking for a bit of insulation—the contemptible tourist bubble, in fact. Traveling alone to a part of the developing world I'd never been to before had me a little edgy, and I'd promised everyone who cared that I would take no chances. So for my first night, I submitted myself to the care of those who are used to looking after anxious northerners.

The blast of cold air when I opened the door of my room was like a breath from the first world. I opened the mini-bar, poured myself a gin and tonic, and sat down to have a little think. It's so easy to be in "solidarity" with the third world (or "two-thirds world," if you like) from the comfort of home. Of course, there are those who genuinely love being in poor countries, who "go native" immediately, at least inwardly. I'm not one of those people. Once actually there, I'm pushed to confront my apprehension, my wealth and privilege, and my dependence on a level of comfort unknown to the people around me. In short, the role of enlightened spokesman for the poor becomes impossible to play, and I am forced to see myself for the first world princess that I am. It's not reassuring. And I haven't even left the hotel yet.

Having gotten this far by thinking, I decide it's time for a shift in strategy, and turn to pray. But prayer is going to be different here. This isn't a place of green pastures and still waters; here I'm going to be wrestling with angels until dawn, and come away limping if I'm lucky. I close my eyes and bare my fear to God, who is merciful and places on me only one expectation: radical openness. This mysterious phrase had haunted me on my retreat a few months before, and although I could speculate a little at the time about what it might mean, eventually I'd had to file it away under the heading, "bound to become clear later." And so it did. I understood that night that any and all feelings I might have about the experiences to come would be acceptable, as long as I didn't run away from them. So long as I remained open to the people, the conditions and the stories I encountered, and didn't turn away, hiding in my hotel room and waiting for the trip to be over, I wouldn't fail. I promised to try.

The next morning I met my driver, Ennis, in the lobby, and we jumped into an air conditioned Alfa Romeo and set off for Elmina. That was when I went into third world shock. This is different from culture shock, because it's not so much a reaction to different ways as to different conditions—specifically, conditions of extreme poverty. My first email to the folks at home began,

> Oh my God. I thought I'd seen the third world before. Turns out I hadn't seen anything, not until today.

I was completely unprepared for the intensity of Ghana. The miles of people outside Accra selling every conceivable product from goats and chickens to soap and toilet paper, both on the side of the road and in between the lanes of traffic. Even children, even at night. The crumbling concrete buildings, which looked liked they'd been burned out and abandoned decades before, though people were still living and working in them. Most of them were missing walls; the two story buildings seldom had a roof. No windows, except on the fuel stations owned by multinational corporations. Many local entrepreneurs operated from a "building" consisting of four twisted wooden poles tied together and covered with dried palm fronds; others were lucky enough to be housed in shipping containers. But most of them had religious slogans on them, usually Christian but some Muslim: "The Lord is My Shepherd Hair Salon"; "Shoes—Blessed are the Merciful"; "Latest Fashions—Inshallah."

Once out in the country, the main difference was a decrease in population density, though in the villages the houses were often made of mud or entirely of palms. We passed a group of women dressed in black, and I asked Ennis about them. He said they were refugees from Chad, who'd come when their country had "a hunger." I later saw a news report on the groups of Sudanese refugees streaming into Chad to escape the violence in their country—what chance do they have, when their refuge is itself pouring out refugees? Shortly afterward we passed through a Liberian refugee camp. My seatmate on the plane had told me that not only had these people lost their possessions and their families, but so many of the women had been raped that the entire female population was deeply traumatized. He said that sometimes when a pregnant woman showed up at a checkpoint, the soldiers would take bets on the sex of the child, and cut the mother open to determine the winner. Impossible not to think of another victim, dying in the sun while the soldiers gamble to pass the time. But there was no time to reflect on this, because each impression was quickly succeeded by new ones.

We passed a man on the roadside holding out a couple of animals upside down. Ennis identified one as antelope, and the other as "grasscutter," or "bushrat." He said he was trying to give up bushrat, because hunters don't always shoot them—sometimes they poison them, and so many people have died from eating the poisoned ones that it's become a public health issue here. I wished him luck, and promised the folks at home that I am not tempted by bushrat.

After three hours we reached Elmina, and my more modest hotel. This time the air conditioner was off, and my room felt like the locker of a very dedicated jock. I managed to get it cooled off somewhat before the power went out; I'd been warned that power outages were a regular feature of Ghanaian life, and while there were no promises, they usually didn't last too long. It didn't this time, which was fortunate because it was too late to go to the castles, so I had nothing to do but hang out and try to process what I'd seen. When the power stayed out longer the next night and left me in complete darkness, I dealt with it by saying evening prayer, which is all about light: *O gracious Light, pure brightness of the everliving Father in heaven. . . . For mine eyes have seen thy salvation . . . a light to lighten the Gentiles, and to be the glory of thy people Israel.* After the Creed and the Lord's Prayer, we pray: *Lighten our darkness, we beseech thee, O Lord: and by thy great mercy defend us from all perils and dangers of this night. . . .* I swear that when I prayed this, the lights came back on—just in time for *Almighty God, Father of all mercies, we thine unworthy servants do give thee most humble and hearty thanks for all thy goodness and loving-kindness. . . .*[1] There are times when it's useful to know something long by heart, and evening prayer helped me stave off nerves when there wasn't a sliver of light in the room, and the air was getting hotter and stuffier by the minute. It was like getting sucked into an overheated vacuum cleaner, but of course, that's just ordinary life for most people in Ghana.

Over the next few days, images of slavery were added to the gallery already taking shape in my mind. At Cape Coast Castle, the tour started in the men's dungeon. This was right under the Anglican church—a nice touch, I thought. The guide pointed to a mark on the wall, about two and a half feet off the floor. He explained that when the dungeon was excavated, from the floor to this mark was a mixture of old chains and shackles and solidified human excrement. At Elmina, the guide took us into the women's dungeon and pointed out that there were places in the corners where the captives were meant to "ease themselves," but that after their forced march of one- to nine-hundred kilometers from the interior, most were too weak to do anything but relieve themselves where they were. Of course, some of the women were still healthy enough to be menstruating, adding to the mix in which everyone slept. Periodically, the women would be paraded naked before the governor of the castle. When he'd made his selection, the soldiers would clean her up and give her enough food to keep her from passing out. Then they'd send her to the governor's quarters; she'd be returned to the dungeon afterward. Women who resisted the sexual advances of any authorities were put into special cells, and subjected to even worse conditions than before. Men who resisted captivity were locked into the "cell of the condemned," where they were left without food, water or ventilation until the

last one was dead. Only then would it be considered safe for the
guards to go in and remove the bodies.

My tour group at Elmina included an Italian man, a farmer,
who spoke no English. The tour took twice as long as it would
have, because everything had to be translated for him, but I appreciated it because I found his interpreter's Italian easier to understand than our guide's English. When we reached the Dutch
Reformed Church, our guide joked about how the Europeans
thought that since they kept their God in this room, he wouldn't
see what was going on outside. At this point, the Italian stopped
the guide and demanded to know: "Where was God when all this
was going on?" The guide shrugged, but he was not to be
deterred, and kept asking, in ever angrier tones "*Where was God?*"

I wanted to answer him. I wanted to tell him that God was
here, in this place, being raped and branded and shackled, forced
to lie on bricks covered with excrement and vomit and blood.
That God wept and agonized with every single soul who passed
through this place, and that he subjected himself to the full weight
of mankind's brutality because of his immense, immeasurable love.
That he holds all the suffering and grief of the world in his heart,
where his touch is the only thing powerful enough to heal wounds
as deep as these. And that this healing is something of what is
meant by redemption: a love so powerful that it can right the most
grievous wrongs. "In the world you face persecution. But take
courage; I have conquered the world" (John 16:33). I wanted to
tell him all these things, but I don't know how to say them in Italian. I wonder if he would have heard them if I had?

My work completed, I returned to Accra. On the way out of
Elmina, the car swerved suddenly, and I saw what Ennis had
avoided: a little goat someone else had hit, lying in a pool of
blood, its legs kicking in pain. I had wept plenty over the past few
days, but privately, in my room. After all the human misery I'd
seen and heard about, it was this little goat that brought waves of
nausea, and tears that could not be put off. I used to feel guilty
about my response to animal suffering, because it seems out of
proportion: at an irrational, gut level not calibrated to my values,

it gets to me in a way that human suffering doesn't. But now I just figure Francis would understand, and I'm sure he would have wept with me over the dying goat. And the Father, who notices every falling sparrow—surely he shared my grief too?

In Accra, I used the last of my emotional energy to look up a fellow Franciscan. I went to his house, and drank his tea while he talked about the challenges of getting local Franciscans together for fellowship. Transportation and lodgings are expensive, and the members are mostly old and infirm. But he has a directory for the American province, and knows my name because he prays for me every month. I was humbled by the perseverance of this elderly priest, who is trying to live out his Franciscan vocation in such difficult circumstances. How much I take for granted the convenience of hopping in my car and driving to our fellowship meetings. I left him with a donation from the St. Clare fellowship, and wished him peace.

Back in my room, I put on the BBC World News while I packed my suitcase for the evening flight back to London. I heard the story of the Sudanese refugees, then another about young girls from Nepalese villages being carried over the border into India and put to work as prostitutes. Human trafficking is one of the fastest growing crimes in the world, the report says, and girls as young as nine years old are being forced to turn up to thirty tricks a day. If they resist, they are tortured. The third story in the series was about AIDS orphans in rural South Africa, some of whom live in villages where there is scarcely an adult left. Weeping has become so routine that I just keep packing.

Later, though, I try to pray. And once again, as throughout this trip, I find it hard to experience prayer as an exchange of love, because I feel the pressure of the suffering I've seen, and haven't resolved the question of how I'm supposed to respond to it. It seems to me that the priorities of an authentic response would be two-fold. First, and most urgently, I need to take action that will really help, not just soothe my own conscience. A response that's all about my internal comfort level is no response at all. But second to that is the very real and legitimate question of conscience:

how do I respond in a way that is faithful to the call of Christ and the way of St. Francis, to the person I'm supposed to be in the world, a response that allows me to live with myself? All the questions I continually wrestle with under the "simplicity" part of the Rule return, but magnified. Yet they really come down to one question: how can God love me when I live in luxury while others suffer so horribly? Have I been deluding myself? I can't go for a little spiritual joyride and just ignore the questions that are pressing on me so heavily, but I don't know how to answer them.

So I pray about them. And once again the images come, each one hard upon the last: images of slaves, images of refugees, images of child prostitutes, of poverty, of a little goat agonizing in a pool of blood. It's bizarre and kaleidoscopic how they keep reappearing and rearranging themselves. But just when they threaten to overwhelm me, I suddenly see that what I'm experiencing is a glimpse into the very heart of Christ, where all the sorrows and sufferings of the world are gathered together. I understand that whenever we witness the suffering of another in an attitude of radical openness—of *compassio*, not turning away but allowing ourselves to feel something of that suffering—we enter into Christ's own heart. Just as when we suffer for him, we share something of his cross. And despite the fact that we in the Church don't talk about this much, I believe that the more we love him, the more we will desire to enter into his sufferings because, for lack of a better way to express it, we'll want to be in this as deep as he is.

So does shedding a few tears make it okay—make *me* okay? No, nor does the fact of Christ's ability to heal people's wounds make it okay for us to inflict them. "Presumption" is an old-fashioned sin that we don't hear much about these days, but presuming upon the mercy of God is a very dangerous business. My tears don't redeem me; I cannot redeem myself. But to the degree that they signal my openness—to the suffering of others, to the truth about myself, and to whatever action God may command—they are a place to begin.

9

STUDY
KNOWING AND UNKNOWING

> True knowledge is knowledge of God. Tertiaries therefore give
> priority to devotional study of Scripture as one of the chief
> means of attaining that knowledge of God which leads to eternal
> life. As well as the devotional study of Scripture, all [Tertiaries]
> recognize their Christian responsibility to pursue other branches
> of study, both sacred and secular.
>
> —*The Principles of the Third Order of the Society of
> Saint Francis,* Days Seventeen and Eighteen

LET'S ADMIT AT THE OUTSET that Francis was nobody's idea of a
scholar. He received the formal education typical of a boy of his
social class in his day. This consisted of grammar—which included
speaking and writing in Latin as well as the basic grammatical
rules—and religion, which involved the fundamentals of doctrine
along with the Scriptures. He also received vocational training in
the cloth business at his father's side. How long Francis attended
school, or how well he did, isn't known. It *is* known that he dictated most of his writings, and that his scribes occasionally pol-
ished up his work, including his rather shaky Latin. Francis didn't
do a lot of writing, and most of what he did write was composed
toward the end of his life, presumably with an eye to guiding his
followers after his death. But although Francis liked to describe

himself as an *idiota*, or illiterate person, there was obviously a good deal of humility in that description. Francis wrote some profoundly beautiful poetry, especially his famous *Canticle of the Creatures*. A joyful hymn of gratitude for the whole of creation, it was composed during a time of intense suffering and inspired many poets after him, most notably Dante Alighieri.[1]

There have been great Franciscan scholars from the very beginning, of course, St. Anthony of Padua and St. Bonaventure being the most famous from Francis' own day and the next generation. But while Francis revered the learned theologians and sometimes assigned them important positions within his Order, he was deeply suspicious of book learning. He believed that for most of the friars it was a temptation and a distraction, and he didn't want them to fall into the trap of mistaking knowing *about* God for knowing God.[2] A story is told of a novice who'd been given leave by a superior to possess a psalter. The novice wanted Francis' consent as well, and kept badgering the saint for it, while Francis tried to put him off the idea. Finally, exasperated, Francis told him:

> "And when you have a Psalter, you will want a breviary; and when you have a breviary, you will install yourself in a chair like a great prelate, and you will order your brother: Bring me my breviary!" As he said this he was carried away with deep emotion, took some ashes from the hearth, sprinkled them on his head and rubbed some on himself, repeating: "That's the breviary!"[3]

Francis believed that learning, the trappings that accompany it and the structures that support it, are fundamentally at odds with holy poverty, and should be renounced just as the Order had renounced comfortable monasteries and ecclesiastical honors.[4] He said that even the greatest clerics who joined the Order must relinquish their learning as a possession, and come naked to Christ, and he called all his brothers to prefer virtue to knowledge.[5] Yet when gifted intellectuals like Anthony appeared and combined powerful preaching and teaching with great sanctity, it was harder for Francis to oppose academic study altogether—

particularly when additional pressure was applied by the pope. The issue remained a thorny one even after his death, however, when many in the Order distinguished themselves in universities all over Europe, while others sought to retain the simplicity of the founder. "'Ah Paris, Paris!' exclaimed Brother Giles. 'It is you who are ruining the Order of St. Francis!' Later on, the Franciscan poet Jacopone da Todi likewise accused Paris of having brought about the ruin of Assisi."[6]

The quotation from the *Principles* at the head of this chapter confirms that Francis didn't win this battle—at least not entirely: "As well as the devotional study of Scripture, all [Tertiaries] recognize their Christian responsibility to pursue other branches of study, both sacred and secular." Together with prayer and work, study is now one of the three primary forms of service required of all members of the Third Order. The Scriptures have primacy, but Tertiaries are also required to read certain Franciscan materials, including biographies and other studies of Francis. There is also a commentary on the Rule and various aspects of the Franciscan way called *Forming the Soul of a Franciscan*; postulants and novices read a chapter a month from this, and professed members are expected to review it periodically. There are also documents that concern the history and administrative structure of the Order. Beyond these materials, all Franciscans are to study works "both sacred and secular." The secular books I've read in the last month include one on the Rwanda genocide and another on contemporary slavery. Because they push me to enter into the suffering of the poorest people in the world, these books would certainly qualify as appropriate materials for study under the Rule.

Like prayer and work, study is a component of the Rule and can't be neglected, even on the grounds that Francis himself neglected it. At the same time, we can't afford to ignore Francis' warnings about the dangers inherent in the culture of academe: systems of hierarchy and deference, egos jostling for position, knowledge conscripted into the service of ambition, the inversion of priorities that excuses personal cruelty in the pursuit of status. These dangers aren't unique to universities; they exist in every setting where expertise is valued, and in our society, that doesn't leave many settings out. But learning is the coinage of the academy, so it's there that the temptation to self-aggrandizement and the manipulation of others through knowledge are most obvious. Francis was right when he argued that intellectual accomplishment caters to our tendency to arrogance, and all too often stems from our longing for recognition and a corrupt sense of value that's derived from what we do rather than what we are.

But he was wrong if he thought we'd be better and purer if we opted out of formal study altogether, because study can also be placed in the service of love. Especially in our day when cultural diversity and global cultural connections are part of our everyday reality, we need study to love—that is, to understand and respect—our neighbor. How can we claim to love our neighbors when we don't even know if they prefer to be called "Orientals" or "Asians"? What do we imagine our homeless neighbors think of our "love" if we're ignorant of the social forces that contribute to their situations, and are left only with the leading explanation of our individualistic culture: "they must have brought it on themselves"? We can hardly fulfill our baptismal vow to "respect the dignity of every human being" if we don't even know how to address them, and can't imagine how a person bearing God's image could end up sleeping under a bridge. But if we study these questions in a state of spiritual attentiveness we will, like Francis, learn to see people and their situations with greater accuracy, not missing the image of God in the face of the leper.

Study is also important because it both reflects and enhances our love for God. I'm not saying that everyone needs to be a theologian—not being one myself, I can hardly impose that demand on anyone else! But if loving our neighbors means taking them seriously enough to do the work of listening to them, and trying to create an understanding that might bridge the distance between us, surely taking God seriously requires the same kind of effort. This involves, first and foremost, taking the Word of God seriously—the Incarnate Word, the written Word, and the words spoken by the Spirit to our own heart:

we try to bring our minds and hearts into harmony with what
God has said and is saying, in Jesus and in the words of Scripture.
We remember that God made all things by an act of self-communication, and when we respond to his speaking, we are searching
for some way of reflecting, echoing that self-communication. . . .
If God has made all things by the Word, then each person and
thing exists because God is speaking to it and in it. If we are to
respond adequately, truthfully, we must listen for the word God
speaks to and through each element of the creation; hence the
importance of listening in expectant silence.[7]

Listening "for the word God speaks to and through each element of the creation" is something Francis was particularly good
at. And while the masters of the spiritual life through the centuries
have much to teach us through their writings, Francis shows us
how much we can learn just by observing the creatures around us:

His favorite bird was the crested lark, called *lodola capellata* in
Italian. "Sister lark with her little hood," he would say, "looks a
little like us, and with her earth-colored plumage, she urges us
to be satisfied with our poor and coarse habits. She is humble
enough to seek her food in dust and dung. Soaring high (as she
usually does) and praising the Lord with her song in the air, she
teaches us to despise earthly things and to make our dwelling
even now in Heaven."[8]

I wasn't initially drawn to Francis because of his celebrated love
for animals—I was focused on other things about him—but it's
something he and I have in common. I confess that I follow Francis at something of a distance here. I don't pick up worms and
move them tenderly to the side of the road so they won't be
crushed, though I did kick a couple of snails off a path today, and
meditated briefly on how the French, of all people, could eat anything so disgusting.

Still, I've discovered over the past few years that you can learn
an awful lot from a dog. I've had two dogs in my adult life, both

golden retrievers. The first one was named Dylan, after Bob Dylan and Dylan Thomas. (I was constantly having to emphasize this, since at the time we got him there was a particularly egregious bit of TV programming, *Beverly Hills 90210*, with a character named Dylan, and people always thought I'd named my dog after *him*.) I chose my dog Dylan for the reason people always choose golden retrievers: they're gentle and loving, easy to train and love fun games like "fetch." Unfortunately, probably because of some irresponsible breeding, Dylan turned out to be the most un-golden retriever in the history of the breed. He was essentially a rottweiler in a golden retriever suit: pushy and dominant with me and aggressive with other dogs, he was always spoiling for a fight, and his idea of playing "fetch" was to collect the stick and then dare me to take it back.

But God, I loved that dog. He was very protective of me—he might put me in my place, but God help anyone else who tried to mess with me. When I'd leave for work, he'd be there at the window wearing a worried expression that meant, according to the experts, that he couldn't figure out how I was going to cope out there without him. Then when he was about five years old, I boarded him for a couple of days while my husband and I took his mother to visit Victoria, British Columbia. When we got home, I was about to call the vet and ask if I could pick him up, when his assistant called me to say that they had no idea why or how, and they were really very sorry, but my dog was dead. It was the only time in my life that I've been truly hysterical. I loved that dog, and what he taught me was this: you can love someone till it hurts, even if they're not very well behaved, even if they have a difficult personality and their habits drive you crazy. It was a time in my life when I needed to learn this, because I figured that to God, I looked a lot like Dylan. And if I could love Dylan that much, maybe God could love me, too.

When the time came to get another dog, I opted again for a golden retriever, though I went for a girl this time. Having learned my lesson, I went to a responsible breeder, one who could provide medical information back through multiple generations, and who did temperament testing. I requested an animal with a personality technically known to dog people as "sweetie pie," and that's exactly what I got. We named her Aberystwyth, after a town in Wales where I've spent time doing fieldwork, but her friends call her Abby. Abby is like furry sunshine; when she's happy she wags her whole back end, and she's always happy. She's not terribly bright, but she too has taught me something important. Abby loves to play, and she gets the whole "fetch" thing. But when it's not play time, she's perfectly content to just sit quietly and be with me. She doesn't need to be doing anything, she just needs to be in my presence, and as long as she is, it's all right. Abby is a four-legged contemplative, a real natural. I needed her lessons, too, because of my tendency to think I must be doing something to be worthwhile. But my dog possesses what Rowan Williams calls "peaceful worthwhileness,"[9] and it's a sense many of us would do well to cultivate.

You can learn a lot from books, and you can learn a lot from dogs, but you can also learn a lot from learning itself—mainly, how little you know. I've spent a good bit of time in school, and each degree I earned made me feel more ignorant, till by the time I got my PhD I realized I knew nothing at all. Of course, graduate school is mostly about training, not education—in graduate school one acquires knowledge in a specialty, learning more and more about less and less. We focus in on our area of expertise until it's easy to lose sight of the bigger picture: as Marshall McLuhan said, the specialist is one who never makes small mistakes on the way to the grand fallacy. In our world of exploding information, however, specialization is unavoidable, and experts are, after all, useful things to have around.

But I think humans have a natural apophatic tendency—an intuitive sense of the limits of knowledge—and serious study can bring it to the surface. Apophatic theology claims that God is so far beyond human experience and understanding that all positive assertions about God's essence are inevitably misleading, distorting and potentially idolatrous. Instead of making statements about what God *is* (the thrust of "cataphatic" theology), apophatic theology emphasizes all that God is *not*: God is not limited ("infinite"), not subject to death and decay ("immortal"), beyond all description ("ineffable"). Because God so transcends our capacity to know him, apophatic theology stresses *unknowing*:[10] we can do nothing but bow in silent awe before the mystery we cannot begin to comprehend. I confess I'm more at home in the cataphatic tradition, with heavy doses of analogy ("God is *like* a king," "Christ is *like* a bridegroom"). Yet there's that undeniable tendency for each little summit I reach to open up new vistas of my ignorance. This makes sense, because it's only when we push ourselves to the limits of our knowledge that we get a feel for where those limits are. So with all due respect to the seraphic father Francis, I believe study—the right kind of study, undertaken in the right spirit—can actually lead us away from arrogance and into a deeper humility. I expect it would take some doing to convince Francis of that. But if it ever comes to a debate, at least I'll have Anthony and Bonaventure on my side.

Questions for Reflection

1. Think about places where you live and work, as well as our public discourse: the media, political debates and so on. In what ways do you see education and expertise used to manipulate and control others?

2. In your own life, can you identify ways in which learning has drawn you closer to God? Are there ways education has distanced you from God? What makes the difference?

3. Education has become one of the most important factors that define a person's status in our society. Think about how your education—or lack of it—has shaped you. If you're well educated, does this fact give you a sense of security and entitlement in your dealings with others? If you're not well educated, does this create insecurity and discomfort in your dealings with others?

4. We're said to live in the "information age," and certainly our access to information is incalculably greater than it was in Francis'

day. If Francis were alive now, do you think his attitude toward study would be different? If so, how?

5. What are some of the ways you study that don't involve reading text? What kinds of things have you learned from this form of study?

6. Are you more drawn to the cataphatic or the apophatic tradition? That is, do you like to reflect on what God is like, or do you prefer to think of God as unknowable, mysterious? In what ways do you see your preference manifest in your spiritual practice? Might you benefit from exploring the other side?

Steps into Study

1. All Christians should be studying the Scriptures, but the thought of reading the Bible is intimidating to many people. If you're one of them, start in the New Testament with one of the gospels. Get yourself a commentary or handbook to help you across the historical and cultural gap between the world of Christ and ours; I've found Eerdman's commentaries helpful, but there are many choices out there. You might also try Tom Wright's justly popular gospels "for everyone" (*Matthew for Everyone*, etc), or the Conversations with Scripture series, available from Morehouse Publishing.

2. Try reading the biographies and works of some of the great saints. There are numerous biographies of Francis available; you might begin with Murray Bodo's books, which contain both biographies and meditations on the lives of Francis and Clare. Omer Englebert's biography of Francis is a classic and an easy introduction. You might also try books that cover more than one saint: *God's Gentle Rebels* by Christian Feldman includes Francis, Elizabeth of Hungary, Teresa of Avila, Catherine of Siena and others. Of course, some of the saints wrote autobiographies: Teresa of Avila and Therese of Lisieux are excellent choices.

3. Experiment with studying creation. What do you learn from your pets, from the changing of the seasons, from the terrain where you live? Kathleen Norris' book *Dakota: A Spiritual Geography* is

a beautiful example of how much we can learn from the most unlikely landscapes.

4. Humans have had a much greater impact on the created world than we'd had in Francis' day. Reflect on our lack of care for the environment; who is most affected by our failures in this area, and what might be done about it?

5. Read up on a social problem that particularly troubles you: the AIDS crisis, racism, child abuse, drug abuse, crime or torture. Do you sense a call to respond to this problem in some way, and if so, what form might that response take?

6. Return to the question of how your education has affected your social status and sense of self. If you're well educated, reflect on the various factors beyond your control that made your education possible: your parents' education and income, your race, sex, the time into which you were born, and so on. If you're not well educated, you are in a significant sense impoverished, whatever your income. Try placing that poverty before Christ; is there any sense in which it is blessed?

Prayer

Lord, you taught us through your servant Francis that knowledge is valuable only insofar as it leads us to you. I know a few things, and there's a lot more that I don't know. May my knowledge always be put to your service, may my ignorance teach me humility, and in all things may I see, know and love you above all. Amen.

10

WORK
THE JOB SEARCH

Tertiaries endeavor to serve others in active work. They try to find expression for each of the three aims of the Order[1] in their lives, and whenever possible actively help others who are engaged in similar work. The chief form of service which Tertiaries have to offer is to reflect the love of Christ, who, in his beauty and power, is the inspiration and joy of their lives.

—*The Principles of the Third Order of the Society of Saint Francis,* Day Twenty

Service has always been an important part of the Franciscan vocation. Daily work is one way in which Tertiaries serve God and others; we are often also called to serve God and our brothers and sisters in individual ministries, ranging from prayer to social activism.

—*"What the Third Order Rule Is About"*

"WORK" IS A PART OF THE RULE where Tertiaries have lots of latitude, so it's one that requires disciplined attentiveness as we figure out the form our service should take. In *Forming the Soul of a Franciscan*, the commentary on the Rule that Tertiaries study during the formation period and beyond, we're given some guidance. The document notes that Francis' vocation made use of the experiences and skills he acquired before his conversion; as a merchant, he knew how to turn on the charm to sell cloth, and it wasn't that different "selling" the gospel. We too can examine our history and gifts, listening for the kinds of needs that stir us. We consider new invitations to service that arise, as well as opportunities to serve in the places—on the job and off—where we already are. *Forming the Soul* acknowledges that, in spite of this guidance, "Those in formation sometimes find it difficult to know what to do for their rule of work."[2] Our lives must contain some form of work, however; Francis had little time for idleness. To a brother who ate well but refused to share in the labor he said, "Go your way, brother fly, for you want to eat the sweat of your brothers and to do nothing in God's work. You are like brother drone who wants to be first to eat the honey, though he does not do the work of the bees."[3] All Franciscans have some kind of job, and the ones I've known who were disabled or bedfast have worked as hard as anyone.

When I returned to the Church after my years in exile, I assumed I'd be given a job. In Church circles, the kind of job I expected is known as a "ministry," but I dislike jargon, and words like "ministry" tend to make me nervous,[4] so I'll simply refer to what I expected as a job. Everyone else seemed to have a job: people I encountered in my parish were involved in AIDS work, visited those in jail, cooked for the homeless, and tried to keep the youth of the parish from sinking into delinquency. Once I started hanging around Franciscans, the jobs got even more varied and interesting: people were working with immigrants, with prisoners, teaching methods of prayer, counseling couples and families—they all seemed to be busy following the examples of Christ and of Francis, serving the poor, the needy and the vulnerable.

I also thought I'd be given a job because, long before being drawn to the Franciscan way, I had been trained to expect it. The radical Christian group I joined as a teenager taught that the only true job for a believer was full-time evangelism. Coming out of the "Jesus people" movement of the sixties, this group understood evangelism as hanging around on street corners and "witnessing" to passersby. I never thought much of this method, feeling that it likely did more harm than good. In my case, at least, it never did any discernable good, probably because my own reluctance to inflict myself on strangers made me a pretty unenthusiastic evangelist. We never quite sank to the level of the person who sits in the football stadium holding up a sign that says "John 3:16."(I'm not sure what this is meant to accomplish, other than to score evangelism credits that could be used to buy approval from God.) I think much of that type of thing is motivated by fear: "If I don't get the gospel to these people, their lost souls will be on my head, and God won't love me." I understand that fear, because it's been used on me. But I came to see it as deeply misguided.

When I regained my faith in my thirties, I promised myself that I'd never again be pressured into "guerilla evangelism": I'd just be open about my beliefs, and try to live in a way that backed them up. I didn't know it at the time, but this is a very Franciscan approach. Francis advised his followers to "preach the gospel at all times; if necessary, use words." A story is told that Francis and a companion set out once to preach in a particular village. They arrived, and as they passed through the village, Francis met up with several people. He gave alms to a beggar, helped an old woman carry a load, comforted a crying child. When they reached the opposite end of the village, Francis made for the road, when his companion asked him, "When are we going to preach the gospel?" Francis answered, "We did." Francis didn't take this approach because he lacked the courage to speak, or because he was afraid to look foolish in the eyes of others. He took it because it seemed to him the most genuinely effective way to reach people with the love of God. When I heard Francis' advice on evangelism, I felt drawn even closer to this gentle man who, as the *Principles* put it, "reflected the love of Christ, who, in his beauty and power, was the inspiration and joy of his life."

Still, Francis had a job—surely I should have one, too? There were others who led me to believe so. Dorothy L. Sayers is best known for her mystery novels but was also a Christian apologist and possessed a formidable intellect. Sayers wrote extensively of her conviction that everyone has his or her "proper job," the job each of us was meant for, and is called to. Our task is to find that job and do it with all the energy, integrity and passion we can muster. In her finest novel, *Gaudy Night*, Sayers explores this theme through her protagonist Harriet Vane. Torn between alternative callings, Harriet wants to pursue the one of greater ultimate significance, and she asks a don at her old Oxford college, "How can we know when something is of overmastering importance?" "We can only know that," the older woman replies, "when it has overmastered us." We'll know we've discovered our proper job, Sayers maintains, when we find that task to which we cannot bear to give anything short of our best. When no sacrifice is too great, no detail is too trivial, and we're prepared to lavish the last of our resources on it, then we've found our vocation.

Armed with this insight, I began looking for employment. And now I have a new sympathy for that category of people known as "discouraged workers," those who aren't even counted as unemployed because they've given up seeking work. I tried a whole string of worthy causes that were close to my heart, and to which I thought I might be able to contribute something. I kept assuring God that I'd be happy with something very humble and behind-the-scenes, something out of the spotlight, obscure and unappreciated . . . until he made me see that I was making a fetish of obscurity. What if he were calling me to something public? Okay, I said, I can go with public. Public is fine too. And I knocked on one door after another, *and nothing happened*. I joined one group but became increasingly uncomfortable with their methods. I joined another organization and it folded shortly thereafter. I went to a conference and volunteered for a task force that never met. I found occasional opportunities to stuff envelopes, but nothing that seemed like a "proper job," and I was getting worried.

Francis himself struggled with this. There were several critical moments in his life when he was uncertain which direction to take, and even though he was clearly being given directions, he didn't always know how to interpret them. Before Francis' conversion, during one of the skirmishes between the rival cities Assisi and

Perugia, he was taken captive and imprisoned for a year. Shortly after his release, barely recovered from a serious illness, Francis was thinking of trying again for military honors when he had a dream in which he was master of a palace filled with splendid weapons and trappings of war. Taking it as a promise of success on the battlefield, Francis charged off in the direction of Apulia in the service of a great knight, but he was quickly brought up short by a second dream. This time, God asked him who could do more for him, the servant or the lord? "The lord," Francis replied. "Then why are you abandoning the Lord to devote yourself to a servant?"

Realizing that he'd misinterpreted the first dream, Francis returned to Assisi considerably humbled.[5] Back home, he wandered aimlessly in the surrounding countryside trying to "find himself." He sought out places of solitude, hoping for direction, and dramatically received it one day at a little run-down church called San Damiano. Francis was kneeling before the church's wooden crucifix when from it, the Lord spoke to him: "Francis, go and repair my house, which as you can see, is falling into ruins." Again a bit slow on the uptake, Francis took this call literally, and repaired three churches before it began to dawn on him that it was the larger Church he was called to rebuild.[6]

Francis also used the Scriptures to discern his way, though not being a great student he resorted to the medieval equivalent of Cliffs Notes. When he attracted his first follower, Bernard of Quintavalle, Francis proposed they go to a church and consult the gospel regarding what they should do next. They opened it three times at random, and received the following instructions: "If thou wilt be perfect, go, sell what thou hast, and give to the poor"; "Take nothing for your journey"; and "If anyone wishes to come after me, let him deny himself." This method seems to have worked out pretty well for Francis, though I'm not sure I'd rely on it myself. Francis was probably on more solid ground when, after returning from his aborted trip to Apulia, he sought out a confidant in Assisi who was known as a holy man. This seemed to help Francis move closer to determining his purpose in life, so I figured I'd follow his example and, beating back a rising sense of panic, consulted my spiritual director.

"Maybe I'm just unemployable," I suggested. "Maybe I can't be trusted with a job." He reminded me that I was already working pretty hard—after all, I was teaching full-time—and said he thought I was in fact making important contributions. I dismissed this, figuring that he was just setting the bar too low, being lenient with me, like the priest in *The Canterbury Tales*: "Full sweetly heard he confession/And pleasant was his absolution." I brought the matter up in formation class, the monthly meeting in which postulants and novices learn about the Franciscan way, and share their own initial experiences with living the Rule.[7] "What about this 'work' thing? Everyone else seems to be doing some kind of volunteer work, and I'm not doing anything." Nobody leaped out of their chair in outrage that I wasn't doing anything, which I couldn't understand. Finally, another novice, whose paid employment happens to be a very powerful and compassionate form of service, spoke up: "Why do you think you have to be *doing* anything?"

I sat there, stunned. It was in the *Rule*, for God's sake. But I suddenly felt the Rule I'd been standing on jerked out from under my feet. The question went so directly to my most basic assumptions that I had no answer for it at the time, though I wrestled with it later. I debated myself in the grocery store: "My Father is glorified by this, that you bear much fruit and become my disciples" (John 15:8). *Yes, but he said we would do that by* abiding *in him.* I returned to the subject on the way to class: "Because Christ is destitute and suffering in places like Africa and no one seems to care." *Yes, but through your teaching you are already giving some six hundred people per year a close look at that suffering, and you can contribute directly to easing it by your own donations—which, incidentally, could be increased.* Walking the dog, it finally hit me: "Because if I'm not working at something, I won't be building up credits, the suffering of the world will be on my head, and *God won't love me.*"

I'm amazed at how much of our adult life is spent trying to overcome the myriad ways in which we were screwed up in our youth. It seems I had yet to shake off the rather warped version of the Protestant ethic I'd acquired during my days in the commune. I'd simply taken everything they told me about evangelism, and transferred it to other forms of service: there were quotas to be made, and if I didn't work hard enough, there would be no excusing the space I was taking up on the planet. Turning from the Protestant ethic to a Catholic classic, I found some consolation in John of the Cross, whose work on the "dark night of the soul" has kept many a believer from despair. When people are experiencing spiritual darkness, John says, one thing that often happens is that they feel a sense of extreme anxiety that they're not serving God. John's counsel to us is full of trust and hope: Don't panic, he says. Don't struggle against the darkness, because in it God is performing a very special work in you. Submit to that work, and allow it to bring you to a new level of intimacy with God.

When I did that, I realized that God was actually trying to give me a job, only I couldn't see it because it didn't look like my idea of what a "proper job" should be. When I stopped flailing around long enough to look closely at my life, I realized that every time I tried to get involved in work that conformed to my idea of a legitimate calling, nothing happened. But that didn't mean that nothing was happening in my life. In fact, I could see God dramatically at work in my life, but it was in my prayer that this was happening, not in any volunteer work I was doing.

The genius of Anglicanism is that it is both Catholic and Protestant, and thus forms a bridge between the two traditions. Individual Anglicans stand at different points on this bridge, and I am definitely Catholic-of-center, but the prospect of a contemplative vocation made my rather feeble Protestant side rear up. I came up with all sorts of reasons why a contemplative vocation was not my "true" call: "It isn't right to sit around gazing at God all day—remember that part about 'bearing much fruit'?" "Pray, of course—by all means pray, but prayer should be fueling you for action." "So-called contemplatives are just self-indulgent navel-gazers, they don't accomplish anything." "Besides, it's just weird."

I admit that this is an unfair caricature of Protestantism, which has produced some world-class mystics; still, I do find that the contemplative tradition is more developed on the Catholic bank. In any case, it was clear that while my vocation might be more contemplative than I'd been willing to admit, there were also other places in my life where God was acting. A few students out of the annual six hundred did seem to be moved by what they learned about inequality in my courses. They spoke of having "conversions," of seeing things in a new way, and of reordering their lives to reflect new priorities. Meanwhile, I also felt a growing desire to write about my experience of the Franciscan way, and others encouraged me in this. Indeed, the *Principles* (Day Eighteen) support the value of this kind of work:

> As well as the devotional study of Scripture, all recognize their Christian responsibility to pursue other branches of study, both sacred and secular. In particular there are members of the Third Order who accept the duty of contributing, through their research and writing, to a better understanding of the church's mission in the world: the application of Christian principles to the use and distribution of wealth; questions concerning justice and peace; and of all other questions concerning the life of faith.

Prayer, teaching and writing: could this be a life that would be genuinely pleasing to God? My eyes drift from the screen to an icon on my desk, an image of Teresa of Avila. Teresa is one of my favorite saints of all time; in fact, I've long considered that if Francis is my sun-sign, then my moon is in Teresa. I spent years with *Interior Castle* and have found that her insights about prayer more than justify the struggle I've had to understand her.[8] The icon before me is a contemporary one, by Janet McKenzie, and shows Teresa with a pen in one hand and an open book in the other. What it says to me is this: a woman who prays, teaches and writes can please God very much indeed. As a calling, it's not exactly unheard of, and certainly not inferior. This is what's so great about getting to know the saints: they show us how many different spiritual "styles" there are, how many ways there are to glorify God. Someone has said that God is like an infinitely complex jewel, and our real task in life is to figure out which of his facets we're meant to reflect to the world.

Getting to know Francis better helped me come to accept the combination of contemplation and action that constitutes my own vocation. And Francis didn't work it out on his own any more than I did. Like Jesus, Francis tended to alternate periods of intense service with spells of solitude and deep prayer. At one point in his life, however, he considered retiring to a hermitage for the long-term, a prospect that must have been deeply attractive to a man who was rapidly wearing himself out in active service. Uncertain what to do, he called on two of his closest friends, Clare and Sylvester, for guidance: did they believe God was calling him to an exclusively contemplative life, or should he continue to balance prayer with preaching the gospel?

Both counselors returned the same verdict: Francis was to continue to preach, and so the Franciscan way has always incorporated both the contemplative and active elements. Returning to the *Principles* again (Day Thirteen):

> Tertiaries desire to be conformed to the image of Jesus Christ, whom they serve in the three ways of Prayer, Study, and Work. In the life of the Order as a whole these three ways must each find full and balanced expression, but it is not to be expected that all members devote themselves equally to each of them. Each individual's service varies according to his/her abilities and circumstances, yet the member's personal rule of life includes each of the three ways.

The contemplative and active elements are both part of a Franciscan's life, but not necessarily in equal measure, at all times. I get the impression that the Lord isn't nearly as anxious about what I accomplish as I am. Indeed, while Jesus said that his disciples would "bear much fruit," he didn't specify exactly what that fruit would be, or how much is "much," and I suspect that a good deal of my anxiety on this score is simply the influence of a culture obsessed with productivity. But God isn't subject to the Protestant ethic; God isn't subject to anything at all.

"Work" is obviously a part of the Rule that's been a real struggle for me. I've been honest about that struggle because I very much doubt that I'm alone in it, and because discerning the will of God for our life, in this area and others, is so important. The Rule put these questions right in my face, but it turns out that it was the Rule itself that helped me answer them. I complained to another Franciscan that I can't seem to discern my way out of a paper bag, and yet the combination of the *Principles*, the formation class, spiritual direction and studying Francis' life—plus the support of my brothers and sisters in the Order—helped me to discern the work to which God is calling me now. The process has been a messy one, and has acquainted me with many a blind alley. Yet in the end, it was the Rule that helped me find my way home. As for the messiness, I'll close with a piece of advice offered by a Franciscan whose own work I've long admired: "Beware of the call that's too obvious. If it makes complete sense to you, you probably made it up."[9]

Questions for Reflection

1. The word "ministry" literally means "service." What makes a job a *ministry*, or service to the kingdom of God? Does all work have the potential to be ministry? Are there any exceptions?

2. Sometimes a person's gifts make his or her vocation obvious. A gifted singer or artist, someone who's good with children, a brilliant surgeon—all these can easily find ways to put their talents to work for the gospel. But sometimes people seem to be chosen for jobs they're not especially suited to. Neither Francis nor Paul the apostle was a gifted speaker, yet both were called to preach and did so with great success. Teresa of Avila was a beautiful and charming extrovert who was called to a life of cloistered

contemplation. Where do you fall on this continuum? Do your gifts make your avenue of service clear, or is this something you need to discern?

3. Is it possible to become over-identified with a particular form of service, so that it becomes an attachment we hold onto when God is trying to move us on to something else? How would you know if this were happening?

4. What does the process of discernment look like? What have been some of your best and worst decisions, and how did you make them? What do you learn from these experiences?

5. Has your "job" (paid or not) changed over time? Perhaps you've been taking on increasing leadership responsibility, or shedding commitments that don't involve children, or spending more and more of your free time making art or music. Does a look at your service patterns over time give you a greater sense of clarity about your vocation? Sometimes we find out what we're supposed to be doing by taking a good look at what we're already doing.

Steps into Work

1. Francis said, "Preach the gospel at all times; if necessary, use words." Think about your life: home, work, other activities. Do your actions in those settings bring the gospel to those around you? If not, what could you change to move in this direction?

2. Is there an issue you're deeply concerned about, one that seems to be calling for some response from you? Investigate whether God is calling you to some involvement in this area: find out what organizations exist, and whether they need volunteers, publicity, contributions or other help. If there's no organized effort to respond to this problem, consider whether you're the person called to start one.

3. *Listening Hearts: Discerning Call in Community* by Suzanne Farnham is a useful resource for those trying to figure out their vocation. Farnham and her co-authors provide useful questions

and steps for those in a process of discernment, which can be helpful for making other types of decisions as well.

4. When Francis was trying to find his life's work, he sought advice from a fellow Assisian known to be spiritually mature. If you're on the same search, consider meeting with a spiritual director to help you get past your own limitations and hear your call more clearly. Finding a good director can take time; you might ask someone who has one for a suggestion, or consult a member of the clergy. Spiritual directors can be clergy or lay people; some charge for their services, others don't. They have different styles, so it's important to find a good fit. If spiritual direction as such isn't common in your church, you might try simply "meeting with the pastor" or a trusted friend older in the faith. Whatever it's called, this practice is as old as the Church itself. An excellent resource for anyone looking into spiritual direction is Spiritual Directors International: www.sdiworld.org.

5. Whether you're searching for a job or well established in your vocation, don't neglect that form of service Therese of Lisieux called the "little way." This consists of small sacrifices and acts of love done quietly for others. Therese said that "love" was her vocation, and it's one the rest of us can claim as well.

Prayer

Lord Jesus, we long to please you, long to hear the words "Well done." But we don't necessarily know *what* to do. Guide us by your Spirit into the work you want us to do, and in the meantime, help us not to miss the little works that are waiting for us every day. Teach us to lay them at your feet with love. Amen.

11

RETREAT
THE GIFT OF YIHUD

Silent retreats and quiet days provide an opportunity to rest and grow physically, mentally and spiritually. At least once a year, we participate in organized or private retreats.

— "What the Third Order Rule Is About"

I'M INCLINED TO AGREE WITH PASCAL that most of our problems are caused by our inability to sit quietly in a room alone. For most of us, however, it's an academic question, because we're so seldom offered a quiet room in which to try it. Nor do we have the time to immerse ourselves in any quiet we do manage to find. Being in Europe reminds me again of how little vacation time most working Americans get compared to Europeans: two weeks at best, to their six or more. Of course, it's worth bearing in mind that much of the world has more time off than they want, and are consequently starving to death. But for affluent people in an affluent country to have so little time to relax suggests a curious ordering of priorities.

Academics are in a somewhat different position. Not because they work less than others do; most of my colleagues work at least sixty hours a week. But while our salaries are low compared to those of most other professionals, and we all whine about our tiny offices, unmotivated students and the disdain of the general public, the one thing we have that is of incalculable value is autonomy. All other considerations aside, I'm delighted to make a quarter of the average physician's salary, if only because I don't have to be at work at six-thirty in the morning unless I want to. Obviously I have to show up for classes, but I have some control over when those classes meet. Other meetings are just far enough out of my control to keep me in touch with life in what others choose to call the "real world." But much of my work I can do when and where I want, and if I want to take it to a cabin in the woods for six weeks in the summer, I can do so—provided I can afford it.

The academy is also one of the few places where you can find the utterly civilized and biblically based practice of sabbatical, probably the earliest known retreat. While the resources for supporting sabbaticals are fast disappearing in my corner of the academy, most tenured faculty are at least eligible to compete for them, and some do actually take one every seven years. Of course sabbaticals are for work, not for lying on the beach sipping piña coladas, but they do give people the opportunity to focus on their work in less frenzied surroundings. For those of us who aren't eligible for sabbaticals, there is at least the rhythm of the academic year: we knock ourselves out during term time, and catch our breath during the breaks. If you really want to drive us crazy, though, ask us what we do with our summers "off." I've never yet encountered a colleague who took the summer off, but it's true that without classes, life does assume a more human pace for a while.

The point is that in spite of all this, I'm still physically and mentally exhausted by the end of the term, and by the end of my teaching year I'm usually sick as well. What life is like for those managing a relentless work schedule, plus children with all their activities, with a week or two of vacation a year, I'm lucky enough to have to imagine. If that vacation time is spent on more activities with the family, when do people find time to slow down enough to recover their sanity? And, crucially, even if we can find the time, do we have the guts to take it for ourselves? How many of us who have jobs or families, or both, are prepared to announce that we're taking a few days to go sit quietly in a room?

Francis was absolutely committed to this practice; he fiercely guarded his time alone with God, and went to extreme lengths to ensure that he could pass that time uninterrupted.[1] He founded a chain of hermitages in caves around Italy to ensure that he and his brothers would be able to find the solitude they craved. L'Eremo delle Carceri, Alverna, Greccio, Le Celle, Fonte Colombo, Monteluco—the names of his favorite retreats speak of a passionate Italian heart that sought its love in silent, stony places. Thomas of Celano records that Francis

> frequently chose solitary places so that he could direct his mind completely to God. . . . If he began late, he would scarcely finish before morning. He would go alone to pray at night in churches abandoned and located in deserted places, where, under the protection of divine grace, he overcame many fears and many disturbances of mind.[2]

A story in *The Little Flowers* shows how carefully Francis defended his solitude. When Francis arrived with three companions at Mount Alverna, some weeks before he received the stigmata there, he took Brother Leo aside. Telling him to stand in the doorway of the oratory, Francis walked a little distance away and called to Leo, who came running at his call. So Francis said, "Son, let's look for a more remote place, from which you cannot hear me when I call." They finally found a spot for a shelter where Francis could pass the time in solitary prayer, safe from interruptions. He told Leo to approach the spot once each day with a little bread and water, and once at night at the hour for matins. When Leo came near, he was to say, "Lord, open thou my lips." And if Francis answered, "And my mouth shall show forth thy praise," then Leo was to come forward. If Francis didn't respond, it meant that he was too absorbed in prayer to speak and should be left undisturbed.[3]

When I was an aspirant to the Third Order and just beginning to experiment with living the Rule, one of the things that most delighted me was the requirement to make an annual retreat. At a minimum, "[t]he requirement for an annual retreat means a quiet day or silent retreat which optimally should be for a whole day of quiet with a night on either end of it,"[4] although longer retreats are beneficial. Now I had the excuse I needed, and I quickly made arrangements to spend five days at San Damiano, a Franciscan retreat center in the Bay Area run by Roman Catholic friars. I felt I wanted to immerse myself in Franciscan surroundings to get the feel of it, and it was a good instinct. My days had just enough structure to them: Mass in the mornings and meetings with a spiritual director in the afternoon, plus mealtimes. In between I hiked some of the trails surrounding the center, walked the beautiful Stations of the Cross set up in a garden, prayed, slept, and stared into space. By the end of the five days I felt I could have stayed much longer, but I was also ready to go, fully at peace about whatever might happen next.

By the next spring, I was eager to plan another retreat. But having gone my whole life without losing anyone really close to me, suddenly I found myself with a half-dozen close friends and family members who were seriously ill. I discovered that spring that retreats can come to you in disguise: weeks spent with my mother-in-law while she died of cancer provided an opportunity to step out of my ordinary life and into a space that was palpably sacred. My mother-in-law was a deeply devout woman whose faith had been subjected to more tests than most of us see. She ailed and died in that faith, with a dignity and trust that affected everyone who knew her. Because I'd dropped everything to go across the country and care for her, my husband's family seemed to think I was heroically unselfish, but it wasn't like that at all. I think I finally made my husband understand it one night, when I told him to imagine that he worked in a temple, and he'd been given the responsibility of caring for the most sacred objects in it. It was a privilege, not a sacrifice, a small thing but so pure that it filled me with joy.

It says a lot about the kind of person my mother-in-law was that my partner in caring for her was the ex-wife of another of her sons: she wasn't someone you'd let go of just because you'd let go of the marriage. In any case, the time we spent caring for her was sacred because the task we were focused on was sacred. Retreat in this case took me by surprise: it wasn't *not* doing work, but doing *holy* work, that made it a retreat. To be "holy" is to be set apart, and that after all is what retreat is all about: being called apart, separated for the purposes of God. If we could just take seriously the sacramental notion that all our work is holy, then perhaps the peace and attentiveness of retreat would follow us home and transform our ordinary lives as well.

After my mother-in-law died, I kept trying to schedule a more formal retreat, but every time I started planning one someone else fell ill. I began to take it personally, and think that my efforts to take a retreat were becoming a public menace. One attempt after another fell through, until finally I carved out a bit of time in January, just a couple weeks before my profession. Of course, since I had virtually no control over the timing, it turned out to be perfect. A moment as big as that deserves some focused preparation, some "time out" to assimilate what's going on. Someone has claimed that for every year of life you get you need two years to figure out exactly what happened, but I don't think it's evenly distributed. Some days don't require a lot of figuring, but a moment like profession needs at least five days, so I scheduled them, this time at a favorite hotel on the Olympic Peninsula.

Port Townsend is a funky little town, a haven for artists, poets and people in tie-dyed shirts and wooly hats (motto: "Port Townsend—we're all here because we're not all there"). Manresa Castle is a hotel just outside of town; it does look like a castle, a smaller version of something you'd see in the Loire Valley, complete with turrets. At one time it was a Jesuit seminary, and they say that a ghost is occasionally seen on the third floor. I've read Cl .rles Williams' novels so I'm not prepared to say there's no such thing as ghosts, but I figured the Jesuits must have left enough good juju behind them to deal with any wandering spirits, and anyway I've always loved the place. So I settled into my little mountain and water view suite, feeling that if this was a long way from one of Francis' austere hermitages, perhaps he'd look the other way since all the local retreat houses had been full.

The degree of structure this time was very different. The first twenty four hours, from the evening of arrival to the next evening, were totally structured by a set of instructions I'd received from the Order. These included the Offices of morning and evening prayer, as well as the "little Offices" of noonday prayer and compline, plus a series of meditations on various Scripture readings. In between these I could walk, nap or write in a journal, but I was advised not to read. I found this directive a challenge, and when a couple of people asked me the reason for it, I had no answer. Nor did most of the meditations speak to me particularly, but there's a time to ask questions and a time to just file it under "obedience" and carry on. I did read during mealtimes, but then, rigidity is not really a Franciscan thing.

Once that period was over, there was no structure to my days at all. At first I found myself disoriented by this, and began to fear that I'd have come all this way and paid all this money only to stare at the four walls until I lost my mind. Then it occurred to me that I was sounding disturbingly like the children of Israel when they complained to Moses, "Is it because there were no graves in Egypt that you have taken us away to die in the wilderness?" (Exodus 14:11, NASB). Francis, after all, had spent forty days on an island with two loaves of bread and nothing to "do," so I decided to stop whining and see what happened. It turns out that retreats are like vacations in one respect: while a short break can help, it really takes a couple of days to settle into a different mindset and a different pace. By the third day I'd started spending most of my time on the beach, and I discovered that the wildness of a nearly unpopulated Northwest beach in January is conducive to a deep inner stillness and attentiveness. It's also cold enough to freeze the marrow in your bones, but that was less important at the time.

Once I found that place of stillness, I was struck by the image of retreat as *yihud*. Yihud is a traditional part of Jewish weddings, in which the bridal couple take a little time out, between the ceremony and the festivities, to be alone together in a quiet room. Pascal would approve. It's an opportunity to assimilate what's happening, and the significance of it, and not allow the day to become a blur as it too often does. In ancient times, when weddings went on for several days, the yihud was the point at which the marriage was consummated. Now, couples may break their fast, or just spend a few moments paying attention—to each other and to the event. The image was especially delightful to me since I was preparing to make lifelong vows, and my retreat gave me a "time out" to reflect on what that would mean. But the image of retreat as yihud points us to the importance of taking time to reflect and assimilate in any significant point in our lives, whether we're embarking on a new relationship, a new course of study, changing jobs, discerning a call or making a weighty decision of any kind. Perhaps what yihud really does is to create a space for God at the wedding; likewise, a retreat opens up space in our lives for the Spirit to be present, and to communicate to us the significance of what we're going through.

When we step out of our ordinary lives long enough to find the stillness and attentiveness we crave, can we take it with us? I think the answer is a qualified "yes." The dentist's office is perhaps an unusual place to experience inner peace, which is why they're well supplied with drugs to drag you to it if necessary. But shortly after my retreat, I went through an entire dental appointment so composed that my dentist commented on it: "You look very . . . *contemplative*, sitting there." Once we've found the interior silence, we at least know what it feels like, and we're motivated to return to it. But it's natural that when we return to ordinary life, with its hurried pace and its distractions, we'll lose our peace unless we continually reinforce it. This is where shorter retreats come in.

The Sabbath, the weekly sabbatical, is a short retreat that we Christians have almost completely lost sight of. We're quick to point out that we're not under the law, and that the Son of Man is Lord also of the Sabbath. Of course, we're also free to eat pork, but that doesn't make it a good idea to consume it morning, noon and night. There is a wisdom to the Sabbath that we ignore at our peril, and as I've experimented with including this in my Rule, I've discovered what a joy it is, and how much I look forward to it. It's true that the work is still there when the Sabbath is over, but I find that I don't mind getting up a couple hours earlier the next day if I've truly had a full day off. The alternative is dribbling the work over my whole week, so that even when I do take a break, I'm nagged by the feeling that I ought to be getting it done. Observing the Sabbath is liberating, because there's at least one day when I'm not supposed to be getting anything done. It's also rather subversive: taking a day off each week is placing limits on what I'm willing to give to my job, my house, my vanity or whatever else I might otherwise attend to, and it's saying that those limits are to do with God's claims on my life. In short, it makes us different, sets us apart, makes us in fact holy, which is part of the reason God gave it to his people in the first place.

Beyond the weekly retreat, there are little retreats we can take each day. Most practicing Christians will already be taking some quiet time each day to be alone with God. But beyond that, there are moments that would otherwise be lost to us, which we can reclaim as mini-retreats: time stuck in traffic, sitting in a waiting room, walking the dog, doing the dishes. It doesn't matter what we're doing as long as we can be internally quiet and attentive. I'm especially fond of long flights as retreats—and when you live in Seattle, all flights are long. I once flew from Seattle to Amsterdam without opening my book, a fact my husband still finds disturbing. In particularly stressful times, though, there's nothing like stopping by a church for a while, especially one where the Sacrament is reserved. Yes, I know that Christ is always with us everywhere. But part of our embodied nature is sensing that more strongly in places set aside as sacred, especially where Christ's own body shares the space with us. In the testament he dictated during his final illness, Francis emphasized that this is the best place of all: "Above everything else, I want this most holy Sacrament to be honoured and venerated and reserved in places which are richly ornamented."[5] It may have been the only time the suitor of Lady Poverty ever called for ornamentation of any kind.

The Christian life has been called a journey so often that it's become a cliché. It's a cliché I can't escape myself, though I sometimes want to call it a "safari," the Swahili word for "journey," just to give it a rest. Still, things become clichés because people keep using them, and they keep using them because they're true. It's true that the spiritual life is a journey, and much of it is through the desert. Retreats are like oases, pleasant places to stop and refresh ourselves before going on. C. S. Lewis rightly reminds us that we're not meant to stay in these places permanently—unless we're called to the cloistered contemplative life, in which case the oasis itself becomes the place of struggle. (I wonder what their retreats are like; would they go to a video arcade for a complete change of pace?) But for those of us in the world, retreats are like deep breaths. If you pay attention to how people breathe, you'll notice that it's common to take shallow breaths for a while, and then a deep, refreshing breath that brings the air right to the bottom of our lungs.

Oases, deep breaths—whatever the image, retreats are something we need at intervals to sustain us, and the longer the interval, the more the discomfort builds. When the work threatened to overwhelm his disciples, Jesus told them, "Come away to a deserted place all by yourselves and rest a while" (Mark 6:31). Francis and his followers did the same. In the midst of a busy life with multiple demands, it can take real determination and sacrifice to carve out a few days for retreat. But because servants are not greater than their master, we must find the humility to admit that we too need time out occasionally. Mini-retreats can keep us going until we can find significant time again, but find it we must. Otherwise, the wedding will be over and we will have missed the whole thing.

Questions for Reflection

1. How would you describe the pace of your life: serene, active, busy, frantic, spinning out of control? What about the lives of your family, friends, coworkers? Do you know anyone whose life seems to move at about the right speed?

2. Has the pace of your own life changed? Where is it now? Do you feel that time is your enemy, and that you arrive at the end of

each day defeated? Why does this keep happening to you? Think about it for a while: some of the reasons are probably obvious, while others may require you to go a bit deeper.

3. How do you react to silence? Are you comfortable with silence when you're alone, or do you find ways like TV or radio to fill it up? What about silence when you're with others; do you let it be or try to fill it with words?

4. How much silence is there in your life now? How much solitude? Do you feel yourself wanting more? Could God be calling you to a greater commitment to solitary prayer? If so, what steps could you take to obey this call? Would it take a few small changes, or something really significant?

Steps into Retreat

1. If you've been living at high speed, a seven day silent retreat is probably not the best way to begin. Try smaller steps. Try adding some mini-retreats to whatever prayer time is already built into your day. If you're accustomed to taking some quiet time in the morning, try a short "time out" in the afternoon or evening: just a few minutes by yourself to shut your eyes, still your thoughts and be present to God. Every day is important enough to contain a little yihud.

2. Be alert to opportunities for retreat in times that would normally be wasted: time stuck in traffic, waiting in line or doing household chores. An attitude of retreat can transform these occasions of frustration into oases of peace.

3. Experiment with observing one day of rest each week. Make a commitment to try it for a month, and use that day both to rest your body and refresh your soul. How does this practice affect your attitude toward your work the rest of the week, and your ability to get it done?

4. Attend a Quiet Day. These are frequently offered during the seasons of Advent and Lent, and generally consist of guided reflections interspersed with periods of silence. Especially during December, a Quiet Day can provide a wonderful escape

from the madness and a way to reclaim the holiness of the season.

5. Schedule a few days at a retreat center. At many of these, you may choose to have spiritual direction or not; retreat houses also differ in how much silence they practice, and what liturgy is available and open to guests. It's probably better to go to a designated retreat center rather than a hotel or other secular place, at least at first, because you want something more than a vacation. Take a journal and limited expectations; see what God has to say to you once the external noise has been stilled.

Prayer

Oh God, you are always calling us into intimacy with yourself, and yet our lives are full of distractions. We long to be alone with you, away from the crowds and the noise and the demands—though to be honest, we're a little nervous about it, too. The idea of spending six months a year in a cave as Francis did is a bit more than we're ready for, but we feel you pulling at our hearts. Teach us to sit quietly in a room alone with you. We'll start with a few minutes today. Amen.

12

PROFESSION
PLEDGED TO THIS WAY

My brother and sister, what do you desire?[1]

I LOOKED OUT OVER THE CONGREGATION: quite a number of people, including some of those I love most in the world, had gathered to hear the two of us make our profession vows. It was a joyous moment—the culmination of years of active and intense discernment regarding our vocations. Becoming a member of the Third Order, Society of Saint Francis in the Province of the Americas involves a structured process of discernment that takes a minimum of three years. During that time, the focus is on discovering whether the person has a vocation to the religious life, to the Franciscan way, and specifically to the Third Order. Here's how the process works.

Upon contacting the Order, the inquirer receives some information and application materials.[2] The application consists of a personal history form, a spiritual autobiography, and instructions for developing an initial draft of a personal Rule of life containing the nine required elements: Holy Eucharist, Penitence, Personal Prayer, Self-Denial, Retreat, Study, Simplicity, Work and Obedience. The aspirant sends in these materials and tries living with the Rule for a few months, while also reading up on St. Francis and on the discernment process. Once the application has been accepted and the Rule approved, and the aspirant has submitted the first monthly report on how he or she is doing with each part of the Rule, then the applicant becomes a postulant.

Postulancy is a period of continued discernment lasting at least six months. The postulant continues to live with and refine the personal Rule and to report monthly to a formation counselor, typically by mail or in a formation class. The postulant works with the counselor in studying formation materials, and also meets regularly with a spiritual director, as well as the local fellowship group where possible. This is a trial period, during which the postulant and the Order try to determine whether they are right for each other. At the end of six months, if recommended by the formation counselor, the spiritual director and the convener of the local fellowship, the postulant may apply for admission as a novice.

With novicing, the person formally becomes a member of the community. The novice promises to follow his or her Rule of life and the *Principles* of the Order, and to continue the formation process for a period of one year. After a year, the novice and the others involved in the formation process review the Rule and the novice's progress. After another year and a minimum of twenty-four monthly reports, the novice may apply for life profession. Another assessment involving the entire formation team is made, and a ballot is compiled and considered by Chapter, the governing body of the province. If elected to profession, the person receives a mandate and then makes his or her life profession to the community. My fellow candidate for profession and I had been through this process together. We'd done our monthly reports, attended our classes and fellowship meetings, conferred with our formation counselors and spiritual directors, written and solicited letters regarding our progress, and taken retreats to figure out, if possible, where we were going and whether we should continue— whether, indeed, we'd be allowed to continue.

But we had been allowed, and now the moment had come. I looked back at the convener of the St. Clare fellowship:

I, Susan, desire to serve our Lord Jesus Christ by Profession in the Third Order of the Society of Saint Francis, for the rest of my life, in company with my brothers and sisters.

I'd had an episode of cold feet that morning; how appropriate, I thought, to have something akin to wedding day jitters. It's not every day that you get up in front of a crowd of people and promise to do something for the rest of your life. Weddings are like that, and so are ordinations. Of course, all of us who are baptized have either done this ourselves, or had it done on our behalf. I don't imagine babies are subject to christening day jitters, though I'm sure their parents are. My parents were of the "let them grow up and decide for themselves" school, and so didn't have my sister and me baptized. By age eleven I had decided this was tantamount to child neglect, and made arrangements on my own to be baptized, just in time to be confirmed along with my classmates. In deference to my evangelical best friend, I requested that the baptism be by total immersion—not an easy thing to accomplish as an Episcopalian, since our churches don't have walk-in fonts. But the priest in charge of the youth of our parish had unusual courage, and agreed to perform the baptism in a mountain river, despite the fact that it was December and it felt like we'd been thrown off the *Titanic*. Had we frozen to death in that river, I'm sure our souls would have flown straight to heaven, since I was newly baptized and he could pass for a martyr.

I made promises that day, in front of the few hardy souls who'd shown up for the occasion, and like others, have had the opportunity to renew those vows periodically in the years since, especially at other baptisms. We confess our faith, promise to renounce evil and put our trust in Christ. We vow to respect God's image in every human being, and to repent and return to Christ each time we fail. What is there left to promise after that? It would seem that our baptismal vows pretty much cover the Christian life, so what is the point of a Tertiary's profession vows; are they some kind of "extra" promises, those reserved only for a spiritual elite, those who were "really serious" about their baptismal vows in the first place?

Clergy and religious have been seen in those terms at times, but I don't know that anyone has ever extended the view to members of third orders. It's an attitude utterly incompatible with the Franciscan emphasis on humility; besides, it completely misses the point. The point of making these vows is not to say, "I'm going to journey farther toward Christ than others," but rather, "I understand that, on the journey I share with all believers, I am meant to take *this* path." One thing that tends to distinguish profession vows from marriage vows is the sheer amount of formal, structured discernment and preparation that goes into them. But profession vows are different from baptismal vows primarily in their particularity. I'd already promised to follow Christ for the rest of my life. At my profession, I promised that I would follow him on *this* path, with *this* community, under *this* Rule. I would take Francis as my mentor and guide, and his path would be my path, his spiritual style my style.

There are those who would be uncomfortable with this, sensing a hero-worship verging on idolatry. But leadership and mentoring in the faith have been a fact of life from the beginning of the Church: as St. Paul wrote to the Corinthians, "Be imitators of me, as I am of Christ" (1 Cor 11:1). I'm not dismissing the dangers of blind submission to corruptible leadership; I've seen those dangers at first hand. But I'd venture to say that I'm in a safer position even than the Corinthians, in that my mentor, being dead, is no longer in danger of corruption. Be that as it may, St. Paul also pointed the Corinthians to the richness and diversity of ways to serve God: "There are different kinds of spiritual gifts but the same Spirit . . . the same God who produces all of them in everyone" (1 Cor 12:4, 6b). Some of the most off-putting movements in the Church throughout its history have been those that proclaimed themselves as "the way," but this is not what profession is about. Profession as a Franciscan is saying, principally, "Out of the multitude of spiritual styles that are pleasing to God,

I've discerned that this one is for me, and I pledge myself to it with the same passionate love and energy with which Francis himself did." The Franciscan path is not "the way"; only Jesus is the Way (John 14:6).

Still, you've got to admire a spirituality that counts joy among its central characteristics, and the visiting friar who preached at my profession embodied this joy in a way that knocked us all out. I'd never before heard a sermon that kept an entire congregation laughing from start to finish while imparting a serious message, but I did on that day. I remained delighted right up until the moment before the Eucharist when the celebrant informed us that my newly professed brother would be distributing the Host, and I would be administering the chalice. The first thing that happened was that the bread slid off the paten all over the floor. Right, I thought, clutching the chalice—all I need is to end up with the blood of Christ all over my chest, and the evening will be complete. But we got through it without further mishap, and moved on to the party. There was cake, and there were gifts. I had promised to bring the champagne, but decided instead on Prosecco, the Italian equivalent, in honor of our roots.

In the midst of the festivities, though, I remembered *yihud*, and paused for a moment to take in what had just occurred, and the vows I had made:

> *I, Susan, give myself to our Lord Jesus Christ, to serve him for the rest of my life in company with my brothers and sisters in the Third Order of the Society of Saint Francis, according to the Principles of the Order, seeking to spread the knowledge and love of Christ, to promote the spirit of love and harmony as the family of God, and to live joyfully a life of simplicity and humble service after the example of Saint Francis.*

A woman came up to me during the reception—someone who'd been attending our meetings, and considering whether the Franciscan way might be for her. She tilted her head: "You know how you got up before God and everyone, and made all those promises about things you were going to do for the rest of your life?" "Yes?" "Well," she said, "that was kind of scary."

Yes, it kind of was.

13

CHASTITY
NOT JUST FOR NUNS

. . . [Tertiaries'] chief object is to reflect that openness to all
which was characteristic of Jesus. This can only be achieved in a
spirit of chastity, which sees others as belonging to God and not
as a means of self-fulfillment.

—*The Principles of the Third Order of the
Society of Saint Francis,* Day Eight

JOINING A RELIGIOUS ORDER AS A MARRIED WOMAN does leave one
prey to endless jokes about chastity. I don't know if single people
get these, but I've had plenty of good natured ribbing along the
lines of "Does your husband know?" My answer is that yes, he
was there when I took my vow of chastity; in fact, he took one at
the same time. We promised God, the priest and all present that
we would "forsake all others" and be faithful spouses, which is
after all what sexual chastity in the context of marriage means.
Outside the context of marriage it's a little trickier: some would
say sexual chastity among single people means no fooling around
under any circumstances, while others would say no fooling around
unless you at least know the person's name, or could identify them
in a lineup.

Notice that I keep referring to *sexual chastity*; this is because
I've learned during the Franciscan formation process that there's a

lot more to chastity than sex. It's not that our sexual behavior is unimportant, far from it. Eros, as we've seen, is an exceedingly powerful force—it's capable of driving us to great good or great evil. Francis, the reformed party animal, wasn't the least bit naïve about the power of sexual temptation, and he went to considerable lengths to protect himself and his brothers from it. In the *Rule of 1221* he commands that any friar guilty of "fornication" be dismissed from the Order, and provides guidelines for avoiding the temptation:

> No matter where they are or where they go, the friars are bound to avoid the sight or company of women, when it is evil. No one should speak to them alone. Priests may speak to them in confession or when giving spiritual direction, but only in such a way as not to give scandal. . . . We must keep a close watch over ourselves and let nothing tarnish the purity of our senses, because our Lord says: *Anyone who so much as looks with lust at a woman has already committed adultery with her in his heart* (Mt. 5:28).[1]

Francis didn't take such a strong position against dealings with women because he devalued them, but because he was realistic about human nature, and we could use a bit of his wisdom today. One time when weakness from fasting forced Francis to pause on a road trip, his companion sent word to a holy woman in the nearest village. She came with her daughter bearing bread and wine, and once strengthened, Francis spoke to them both. He never looked at them directly, though, and when the other friar asked him about this, Francis replied: "Who must not fear to look upon the bride of Christ?"[2] I once saw a woman in a t-shirt with an upward-pointing arrow just under the neck; below it, across the chest, were the words: "I'm up here." She probably would have appreciated being spoken to by a man who was more interested in her heart than the way it was packaged.

To say that there's more to chastity than sex isn't to imply that sexual chastity is unimportant, but that where chastity is concerned, sex is only the beginning—it just scratches the surface, you might say. Chastity is an attitude that we can bring to all human relationships, at all levels, and its essence is a recognition that other people exist for God and not for me. Francis manifested this attitude when he said that a true friar is one who is equally joyful when his brothers respect him and when they reject him, when they beg him to preach and when they boo him out of the pulpit—"*provided that* in both cases the advantage be the same for them."³ That is, a true friar isn't looking to his brothers for approval and recognition, not using them to boost his own self-image. If I adopt a spirit of chastity in my dealings with you, it means that I acknowledge that you're here to serve God's purposes, not mine. You're not a means to any end I might desire; if anything, I'm here to serve you.

I think the first time this really hit home with me was when I had lunch with an old flame a few years ago. The danger that we would fall into each other's arms was nil, but what was more interesting to me was the realization that this was an opportunity to practice chastity at a deeper level. In a situation like that, strokes to one's ego can still be tempting even if more literal stroking is not. It's tempting to want to hear how special one was, how no one else could ever quite compare, even that one has still, all these years and all these miles later, "got it." But as I listened to my friend talk about his life, I was able to say no to these temptations, and give him the sympathetic ear that *he* needed. However much I may have put other people to work on my own projects before or since, this was one occasion when I saw the trap for what it was, and avoided it.

One of the great spiritual friendships in the history of the Church was Francis' relationship to St. Clare. Clare Offreduccio di Favarone, beautiful, noble and barely seventeen, defied her parents and ran away on Palm Sunday to join Francis in following the gospel. In front of her escorts and the rest of the brothers, Francis cut her hair and offered her a rough habit to replace her fine clothing. He then placed her in a Benedictine house where she rode out the storm with her family. She ultimately came to rest at San Damiano, the little church Francis had restored, and in time was joined there by others including her younger sister Agnes and her mother. They became known as the "Poor Ladies," and after her death, the "Poor Clares," the Second Order of the Franciscan family.

Francis and Clare shared a deep intimacy, but they didn't see each other often—certainly not as often as Clare would have liked.[4] In fact, the brothers were surprised that Francis called on Clare and her sisters so seldom, and finally his vicar urged him to have pity on the sisters and pay them a visit. Clare must have been thrilled when he showed up; time would have passed slowly in that place, and here was the man whose charisma had changed her whole life, finally come to speak with them. But she was in for a surprise:

> Francis raised his eyes to heaven, where his heart always was, and began to pray to Christ. He then commanded ashes to be brought to him and he made a circle with them around himself on the pavement and sprinkled the rest of them on his head. But when they waited for him to begin and the blessed father remained standing in the circle in silence, no small astonishment arose in their hearts. The saint then suddenly rose and to the amazement of the nuns recited the *Miserere mei Deus* in place of a sermon. When he had finished, he quickly left.[5]

One would expect Clare to have been bitterly disappointed, and perhaps she was, but she was also greatly edified. She accepted Francis on the terms he offered, and loved him because he served God's purposes, not her own.

It's not hard to find examples to the contrary. I think parents face a special temptation to see their children as means to their own ends: one thinks of the parent who pushes a kid to play football when he really wants to dance, or the student who longs to major in literature but faces pressure from home to do pre-med. Teachers themselves can be guilty of this: one of the things for which I'll always be grateful to my mentor in graduate school was that he never tried to remake me in his own image. This was fortunate for both of us, since we're in fundamental disagreement on most every subject you could name. But I also think it's fairly common for friends to be utilitarian in their treatment of one another, walking away when the other person becomes boring, difficult or a little too honest—in other words, dumping the relationship when it ceases to be rewarding. Chastity insists that being rewarded isn't the point; the point is to help the other to become the person God intends him or her to be. It's hard, because all of us want to feel good, and we want the people around us to make us feel good. But it will be obvious to anyone who's ever seen a crucifix that feeling good isn't what the Christian life is about. It's about becoming Christ-like, and what Christ does is to invite us close, even into his embrace, even when we don't please him at all.

Those religious who have taken vows of *celibacy* often speak of it in terms of hospitality.[6] By forgoing all sexual—that is, exclusive—relationships, they're open and available to all in a way that most of us aren't. This is hospitality at a deeper level than we ordinarily think of it. Usually hospitality means feeding and housing people, welcoming them into our space and caring for their needs. Some people have a special gift for this: we have the good fortune to live next door to neighbors who are also old friends, and they have a genius for making anyone who comes into their house feel like the answer to all their prayers. But I think what celibate religious mean when they talk about hospitality is that what most of us are willing to do at least occasionally with our kitchen, our living room and our guest room, we can also do with our lives, allowing people in, making them welcome and caring for their needs.

This is also a gift, and I'm pretty sure I don't have it. The deeper reaches of hospitality are way beyond me, or at any rate, I can only do this for very few people at a time. I do enjoy feeding people, though: I love to cook, and I love to see people enjoy what I make for them, especially if the meal contains an element of surprise. But there are two traps here, waiting to spring on my unchaste little foot. The first is that when feeding friends or colleagues, the whole thing can degenerate into a performance that has more to do with my ego than their enjoyment. If I'm cooking for the applause first, then I'm not really offering hospitality. I'm conducting a transaction, and Francis taught that those who offered their gifts in exchange for praise were to be pitied.[7] The second trap has to do with feeding the homeless, which I also enjoy doing occasionally. But this too can turn into a feeding of my own ego, if what I'm really about is seeking to establish my status as a "good Christian." If the targets of my "charity" cease to be human beings and my equals, and become my *project*, if they exist mainly to provide evidence of my compassion, I've obviously missed the mark again.

This is hard, hard, hard. Trying to make real human contact across a wide social class divide is incredibly difficult. There was a homeless woman I used to see pretty frequently a few years ago, and we had some interesting conversations. I hoped we might be able to bridge the gap and deal with each other as people, but when one person is broke and the other has money, the roles of pauper and benefactor become virtually impossible to escape. I couldn't see her without wondering what I had on hand to give her that day, and I imagine her thoughts ran on much the same lines. How could it be otherwise? Circumstances forced us into these roles, but they didn't force me to give alms in a way that stripped her of her dignity while building my own self-image. To give in this way is actually taking a great deal more than money, and it's at least as grave an offense against chastity as having a one-nighter with the boss after an office party.

Not that I recommend that. But the Church has a lot to answer for in focusing so heavily on sexual sins that this more subtle but deeply destructive behavior receives little attention. That it has done so is evident in the way people automatically understand terms like "impurity" and "immorality" to refer to sexual misconduct, while seeing "chastity" as no more than the avoidance of the same. I'm guessing that when preachers denounce from the pulpit the falling standards of chastity in our day, they're seldom thinking of the extent to which the standard of living in affluent countries, particularly the low prices for food, clothing and other consumables, directly depends on the low wages paid to the producers both at home and in the developing world. But they should be thinking of it, because this, too, is a sin against chastity, and we're all caught up in it. I wouldn't have nearly the income I do if the people who make my food and clothing were paid what their labor is worth, and I challenge you to find a better example of making people serve my own purposes rather than God's. If the thought of being unchaste on a global level is a little scary, well, it should be.

Ultimately, chastity is about not *using* people, whether for sexual gratification or any other kind of gratification. Using people to prop up my self-esteem, to supply me with cheap commodities, to advance my career or make me feel like a good Christian, would make me "unchaste" if I never entertained so much as a lustful thought for the rest of my life. Francis was a red-blooded guy who, being a vowed celibate, found it healthy not to spend too much time hanging around women. Not having access to cold showers, he was known to fling himself naked into the snow when overheated. But beyond that, Francis found the secret to a deeper level of chastity: it was in seeing Christ in every person he met. The ancient hymn says that Jesus didn't see even equality with God as a thing to be exploited.[8] If we exploit those who bear the image of God within them, then we exploit God himself, and that is truly scary.

My friends tease me about taking a vow of chastity, but it turns out that you don't have to join a religious order, or even get married, to do so. The first and most profound vow of chastity is the baptismal covenant. In the Episcopal Church, we put it this way:

Celebrant: Will you seek and serve Christ in all persons, loving your neighbor as yourself?

People: I will, with God's help.

Celebrant: Will you strive for justice and peace among all people, and respect the dignity of every human being?

People: I will, with God's help.

But regardless of the words that were used, baptism is always a matter of entering into the new covenant with God, becoming part of the Christian community, and taking on the responsibilities that come with the immense privilege of being part of the body of Christ. So you see, everything I've said about the commitment to chastity that I've taken on as a Franciscan applies equally to all Christians. None of us can escape; we are all in this chastity boat together. Keep your hands where I can see them.

Questions for Reflection

1. In his wickedly funny book *Class: A Guide Through the American Status System*, Paul Fussell notes that some people enjoy eating out because they derive a sense of status and privilege from having others serve them. Think about the service people and subordinates in your life. What would it mean to practice chastity in your relations with them?

2. What about those who "serve" us as a nation? Public officials enact policy in our name; military personnel fight wars in our name; prison staff execute criminals in our name, and their colleagues keep the rest in line for us, as do mental health workers. All these people are acting in our name and on our behalf. We may find a lot of what they do distasteful, but they do make our lives easier. Where does the call to chastity lead us in these cases?

3. What about those who make our lives easier because they are undocumented or uneducated and unskilled? We pay less for the products of their labor, and we face less competition in the workplace, because of people like these. Where does the call to chastity lead us in their case?

4. Many Christians are offended by blatant displays of sexuality in advertising and entertainment. But there are more subtle ways in which our society routinely pulls us away from the ideal of chastity. The practice of "networking," for example, involves dealing with others with an eye to what they can do for our careers. What other customs and practices do we take for granted

that put others to work on our own goals? Are these always violations of chastity? What criteria do we use to decide?

5. What about our enemies? Are there ways in which having enemies, whether national or personal, serves our interests? In the Holocaust, Jews were referred to as "rats"; in the Rwanda genocide, Tutsis were called "cockroaches." In what ways are our enemies being portrayed as less than fully human, and how does that serve our interests?

6. Sometimes we let go of relationships for selfish reasons, because they're no longer "rewarding." But are there times when it's appropriate to cut a tie of friendship? What criteria would you use to tell the difference?

Steps into Chastity

1. It's easy to laugh about the women who choose exclusively over-weight friends, to make themselves look thinner. But what about you? Ask yourself: are there people in your life who are there principally because they enhance your image, or make you feel better about yourself? Or perhaps you tend to feel that the people you're close to are a reflection on you, and wish they would speak, talk, dress or otherwise behave better?

2. Spend a few days paying close attention to your conversations with family and friends, whether in person, by phone or by email. Do you ever find yourself drawing the conversation in particular directions, looking for them to accomplish something for you? Try turning it around, and focusing on what you can do for them. Do you feel deprived, or does it feel liberating?

3. Try the above exercise with colleagues and superiors at work. Is it more difficult? Is there a time when "working" these people would *not* be inconsistent with chastity?

4. Jesus gave us a lesson in chastity when he said that we should extend hospitality to those who can't return it. Maybe you aren't ready to invite homeless people to your next dinner party. But could you invite someone you're not really fond of, someone

shy, isolated or of a lower status, who doesn't have the social resources to repay you?

5. By being priced a bit higher, fair trade products such as coffee and chocolate ensure that the producers are paid enough to maintain a decent standard of living. Investigate what fair trade items you could substitute for products you currently buy. Some useful resources can be found at: http://www.fairtrade federation.org/ and http://www.transfairusa.org/.
Co-op America also operates a very useful site that makes it easy to find out about the companies you do business with: http://www.responsibleshopper.org/.

Prayer

Oh God, you created us in love and for love. You didn't *need* us to do anything for you. But we are full of needs, and insecurities and desires. We want so much that we aren't content to work on our goals ourselves; we keep putting others to work on them too. Teach us to rest in your loving care, to trust you for our needs, and to spend ourselves in the service of others, because it is there that we most perfectly serve you. Amen.

14

OBEDIENCE
THE ENEMY OF FREEDOM?

All Tertiaries are obedient to the decisions of Third Order Chapter. We say the Daily Offices, we support each other by prayer, attendance at Fellowship meetings and a pledge of financial support to the Third Order. We report regularly to the Order on the keeping of our Rule. We have Spiritual Directors whom we see a minimum of twice a year.

—*"What the Third Order Rule Is About"*

IT'S PROBABLY JUST AS WELL that "obedience" is listed at the very end of the Rule, because it's about the last thing most of us want to hear. In Western culture, perhaps most noticeably in America, freedom and individualism are highly prized; indeed, it would be hard to name ideals that are more valued than these. Freedom is probably the one thing the majority of Americans would say they cherish most about their homeland, and justly so: though we're hardly the only nation where people are free to speak, read, worship and associate as they please, America is different in that freedom was its original reason for being. So why would a twenty-first century American take a vow of obedience? Perhaps this is just a vestigial bit of medievalism in the Rule that ought to be allowed to wither away. Or perhaps it just needs a bit of updating. We could rename it so that it would be more attuned to contemporary sensibilities: how about "Checking In"? To date, however, obedience remains a part of the Rule, and taking a vow of obedience is probably one of the most countercultural things an American of our day could do. Why do it? And what, in the context of the Third Order, does such a vow entail?

Before answering these questions, we might pause to consider what we mean by "freedom," and the relationship between freedom and individualism. Our concept of freedom as the absence of constraints on the choices and behaviors of the individual is both time- and culture-bound. As Orlando Patterson points out,[1] in the ancient world no one would have defined freedom in this way. The normal condition of existence was for each person to be part of a web of culturally defined, reciprocal rights and obligations—in short, to be part of social life. This is why Patterson defined slavery as "social death": slaves were those torn out of that web, whose relationships had no legal standing, who had no one whose socially recognized duty it was to help them. Conversely, free persons could draw upon others who were obligated to them, but they also were obligated to others in their turn. Thus to be free in these terms isn't to be unaccountable to others; it merely means that others are also accountable to you. Variations of this understanding of freedom are also present today in other, less individualistic societies than our own.

So let's acknowledge at the outset that our idea of freedom is one that would be considered eccentric by most of the human race, for most of our history. But we like it, because it means two very pleasant sounding things: I can do what I like, and no one can make me do what I don't like. In practice, of course, the social contract means that we all agree to certain restraints on our freedom, which make social life possible: I'm not free to commit murder or drive on the wrong side of the road. If I pretend that I am, the state will sanction me accordingly. But apart from those limits that prevent society from degenerating into chaos, and despite the fact that our reality is in fact a web of reciprocal rights and obligations, our culturally defined ideal is the absence of constraints. This is why, if you can't be independently wealthy, the next best thing is to be self-employed, and we envy those exalted creatures, the celebrities, who never have to wait behind others for a table. Adolescents long to be free from their parents, little dreaming how un-free adulthood can feel. And many people, if they think of finding God at all, would rather find him in the woods, on the beach, at the golf course, or anyplace other than a community where they might wind up face-to-face with a hierarchy and a set of rules.

I confess that those are my inclinations, too. I'm not a natural joiner, and generally dislike having to show up for things. I would have been in my element in the old West, where if you could see the smoke from your neighbor's chimney he was too close. And one of the things I like best about my job is that very seldom does anyone actually tell me what to do. Despite my obvious temperamental unsuitedness, however, I have somehow embraced Christianity—a religion that doesn't really indulge my natural inclinations much. It not only expects me to actively participate in a community, but also places constraints on my behavior, and makes me accountable to others for that behavior: "Obey your leaders and submit to them, for they keep watch over your souls as those who will give an account. Let them do this with joy and not with grief, for this would be unprofitable for you" (Hebrews 13:17, NASB).

Francis was adamant about this. He insisted that he would obey a novice who'd been in the Order a single hour if that novice were made his guardian, as willingly as if he were the oldest and holiest friar in the Order, adding that the shortcomings of a superior only increase the humility of the one who obeys.[2] Like Jesus, Francis knew the value of dramatic imagery for making a point stick, and he likened the truly obedient person to a dead body:

> Take a corpse . . . and put it wherever you like. You will see that
> it does not object to being transferred, does not complain about
> where it is put, and does not protest when cast aside. If you set
> it on a throne, it will look down, not up; if you dress it in royal
> robes, it will only seem paler than ever. A person like that is truly

153

obedient; he does not mind where he is put, and he makes no effort to be sent elsewhere. If he is promoted to office, he preserves his humility, and the more he is honored, the more unworthy he thinks himself.[3]

Francis not only expected members of the Order to "honor [the guardian of the Order] as Christ's vicar,"[4] but they were to reverence all priests, as he himself did:

[E]ven if they sought to persecute me, I would nonetheless return to them. And if I were to have as great a wisdom as Solomon possessed, and were to meet with poor priests of this world, I do not wish to preach without their consent in the parishes in which they dwell. And these and all others I desire to reverence, love and honor as my lords. And I do not wish to discover if they are sinners, because I behold in them the Son of God, and they are my lords. And for this reason I do this: because in this world I see nothing with my bodily eyes of Him who is the most high Son of God except His most holy Body and His most precious Blood, which they receive and which they alone minister to others.[5]

Well, naturally Francis hadn't been treated to scandal after scandal involving the most predatory abuses by these "lords" of the trust that was placed in them. But I have. Like everyone else, I've read the news accounts, but I have also seen for myself, up close and very personal, the destruction that ensues when spiritual authority is abused. As C.S. Lewis said, "Lilies that fester smell worse than weeds"[6]: it is the highest and noblest things that are the worst when they're corrupted, and religion, which treats of the highest and noblest things, is the most corruptible force on earth. The cop who writes an unfair traffic ticket is annoying, but the cleric who threatens eternal damnation can do far more damage. I've known people so manipulated by the illegitimate exercise of religious authority that they've suffered emotional breakdown, fractured families, loss of faith and physical assault, including rape.

And those are just the ones I've known personally; well documented contemporary cases I've read about broaden the scope to include not only pedophilia but incest, torture and suicide. How can someone who's visited such shady parts of the religious landscape take a vow of obedience to religious authority?

Because obedience to legitimate authority, properly exercised, is a thing of real beauty.[7] Christ himself is our model. He obeyed when it cost him everything; he obeyed when he thought there might be a better way. Of course, Jesus was obeying the Father, not some perverted despot in a collar, or even some unenlightened novice counselor or spiritual director who just doesn't get it. Why is submitting to the likes of them such a beautiful thing? I'll return to the perverts in a moment, but the beauty of obeying when I don't agree, and don't see the point, is in the limits it puts on my ego. It's worth paying attention to my speech, and trying to avoid self-aggrandizement, posturing and one-upsmanship, but ultimately talk is cheap. It's when I give up the need to be in total control of my life, and acknowledge that someone else has the right to speak about how I live, that I begin to "walk my humble talk." Francis used to say that a friar had not given up everything for God if he kept "the purse of his own opinion."[8]

Obedience can be a way of saying, "My ego isn't what's important here. My interests aren't what matter most here." It's a way of preferring others over myself, but it's also a way of acknowledging that leadership is a tough job. Having been in a minor position of leadership in my own parish for a short period, I can say that it's a filthy thankless task, and I wouldn't do it again unless God spoke straight into my ear. Obedience to legitimate authority, properly exercised, recognizes that those who are leading have the hardest job, and the least we can do is try to support them: "We beseech you, brethren, to know them that labor among you, and are over you in the Lord, and admonish you; and to esteem them exceeding highly in love for their work's sake" (1 Thessalonians 5:12–13, ASV).

All right, but what about illegitimate authority, improperly exercised? What about those perverts? First, I must say that the worst cases of abuse I've known occurred because the perpetrators were not themselves subject to effective authority. How this happens depends on the organizational structure of the group in question: some leaders are accountable to no one, while others are accountable to superiors who are willing to cover up for them. But the important question for our purposes is this: how do we know when authority has become illegitimate? At what point does it become our duty to resist rather than to obey? The highest authority in the Anglican Communion is Rowan Williams, the Archbishop of Canterbury, and I recently heard him address this very issue.[9] He noted that Jesus was indeed "obedient unto death," and this obedience cost him suffering that in his humanity he naturally resisted:

> Yet it is a conformity not to some alien authority, to a hostile tyrant in the heavens, but to the root of his own life. He is himself the mind and heart of God; as he looks into the mystery of his own origination in the Father, he acts out who and what he is—the embodiment of the Father's will for the healing of creation. To imitate Christ in his submission is therefore not to do violence to your own proper reality, but to discover yourself as a created being—as a being whose life is grounded in the loving gift of God and nothing else. God's will is that you live; to seek obedience to him is to seek life. . . .

At the political level—and I would extend this to the politics of the Church—Williams argued that Christian obedience can never be a passive, blind obedience. Our attitude is one of "challenging loyalty," one that both seeks and speaks the truth in love:

> It is properly an obedience given where we see authority engaged with a truth beyond its own interest and horizon—ultimately with the truth of Christ. . . . Now we do not usually look in our rulers for signs of advanced contemplative practice; nor do we say, even as Christians, that no obedience is due to unbelieving

governments. But we do say that credible claims on our political loyalty have something to do with a demonstrable attention to truth, even unwelcome truth.

When leaders are inattentive to the truth, when they deliberately distort it or simply ignore it, the better to pursue their own interests, they lose their claim to our obedience. Williams observed that we need not second guess every decision, and that decisions arrived at through some legitimate, "attentive" process may have to be accepted even if we don't agree with them.

Francis' own "process" was sometimes a little dubious. Once when he was traveling with Brother Masseo they came to a crossroad that offered them the choice of Florence, Siena or Arezzo. Masseo asked Francis which road they should take, and Francis responded, "We will take the road God wants us to take." Masseo rashly asked how they would know this, and Francis made him spin around in the road in front of all the passersby, and not stop until he was told. Masseo obeyed, for a sickeningly long time, and when Francis finally stopped him he was facing Siena. So off to Siena they went.[10]

Francis wasn't above issuing orders that he later regretted. Once he sent Brother Rufino off to preach to the people of Assisi. Rufino demurred, on the grounds that he was a simple, ignorant man with no gift for preaching. Because he didn't obey instantly, Francis added that he should go and preach wearing nothing but his breeches. Rufino stripped down and went, to the great amusement of the people of the town. Meanwhile Francis began to reproach himself for giving such a harsh command, so he threw off his habit and joined Rufino naked in the pulpit. He preached so marvelously that the people stopped laughing and repented. Since Brother Leo had sensibly followed Francis and Rufino with their habits, they both got dressed and left rejoicing.[11] Francis wasn't perfect in his exercise of authority, and perhaps making Rufino appear naked before his listeners wasn't the wisest idea—though as a teacher, I know that public exposure and vulnerability are just part of the job. But Francis was a good leader because he loved those in his care. In a letter to one of his ministers, he wrote:

> There should be no friar in the whole world who has fallen into sin, no matter how far he has fallen, who will ever fail to find your forgiveness for the asking, if he will only look into your eyes. And if he does not ask forgiveness, you should ask him if he wants it. And should he appear before you again a thousand times, you should love him more than you love me, so that you may draw him to God; you should always have pity on such friars. Tell the guardians, too, that this is your policy.[12]

As a leader, Francis' zeal sometimes outweighed his good sense. But there is no record of his ever abusing his authority, or exercising it in a destructive way.

When leaders' inattention or resistance to truth results in serious harm or injustice, however, our own faithfulness to truth will require us to oppose them—prayerfully, lovingly, and with much soul searching. Francis cautioned the ministers of the Order not to issue orders that would violate a friar's conscience or the Rule.[13] To the friars, he acknowledged that they might disagree with their superiors and they might be right, but in such cases they should do their best to obey and make an offering of their own will to God. Nevertheless, if a superior commanded something against conscience, the friar was not bound to obey though he should still respect the minister's authority.[14] In the *Rule of 1221*, Francis makes this perfectly clear: "A friar is not bound to obey if a minister commands anything that is contrary to our life or his own conscience, because there can be no obligation to obey if it means committing sin."[15] Of course, all of this begs the question of how much power leaders should have, or indeed, whether the Church should be governed hierarchically, democratically or some other way. These issues have occupied some of the greatest minds of the Church for centuries, but they need not occupy us now. Our concern has been limited to the question of why an individual would voluntarily submit to religious authority, and whether and how just limits might be placed on that authority.

So long as our leaders aren't abusing their power, and so long as they're attentive to the truth and open to our intelligent and informed input, we're probably safe following them—with eyes wide open. What does that mean for Tertiaries, on a practical level? First, because we don't usually live in a physically defined community, the Order has far less say about our lives on a day-to-day level than it would if we were under the same roof, where someone has to decide who does which chores and whether we're all going to be vegetarians or not. At the same time, however, the Rule itself, and especially those elements contained under the heading "obedience," are all designed to build up a sense of community among us. Second, much of our obedience consists in keeping the Rule, and we report regularly on how we're doing with this. But while the nine elements of the Rule are predetermined, and while some parts carry certain minimum expectations (e.g. Tertiaries will be present at the Eucharist at least weekly, and make their confession at least twice a year), mostly we work out the details of our Rules ourselves—in consultation with our spiritual director and formation counselor or chaplain—in a way that works for our own circumstances.

There are, however, certain things that are specific to the obedience part of the Rule, and one of them is the requirement that all Tertiaries be under spiritual direction. Further, it's expected that our spiritual directors are themselves under direction—that our leaders be accountable. This practice was new to me when I started the formation process, though I'd been considering it for some time. I needed some perspective on my life, since it's impossible by definition to be objective about oneself. But I also told my director, when I first approached him about it, that I'd found it was too easy to cut all kinds of private deals with God and then weasel out of them. God, who is well acquainted with my worst side, would not be surprised when I failed—disappointed, but not shocked. Another person, though—that's something else again. This is also, for me, one of the benefits of sacramental confession:

God will understand, but will my confessor?[16] It can be a pretty effective deterrent. There are things I don't do because I don't want to have to confess them. I realize this isn't the most grown-up motivation, but it works, and I can live with being childish about some things if it keeps me out of trouble.

One thing that especially strengthens the Order as a community is our shared life of prayer, particularly in praying the Daily Office together. This discipline is a real challenge for some people, and when he was close to death Francis himself confessed to the entire Order that he had failed to say the Office as the Rule prescribed.[17] As part of the Office, we offer intercession for one another: the directory is divided into thirty groups so that we each have one day of the month in which the entire province of the Order is praying for us. We also read each day from the *Principles of the Third Order*, preceded by Francis' prayer: "Both here, and in all your churches throughout the whole world, we adore you oh Christ, and we bless you, because by your holy cross you have redeemed the world." Tertiaries are also expected to participate, to the extent they are able, in their local fellowship meetings. Some of us live in remote areas and don't have regular access to others, but the local fellowship is the visible Franciscan community for most of us, and being an active part of that is a priority. Further, we're expected to make a financial pledge to the Order—in whatever amount we feel is appropriate—and to keep our payments up to date. This, too, reflects our commitment to the community, "for where your treasure is, there will your heart be also" (Matt 6:21, KJV).

Finally, Tertiaries are obedient to the decisions of Chapter, the governing body of the Order in each province. Such decisions range from the requirement to recite the Daily Office (not required in some provinces), to whether a candidate for novicing or profession is allowed to proceed. So far I've found this to be a pretty easy yoke, but there's no guarantee that that will always be true. One issue that has been under consideration by Chapter for some time is whether to require background checks on all members of the Order. When that decision is made, we'll be bound to comply with it, though there's considerable debate among members and neither choice will please everyone. The arm of Chapter only reaches so far into my life, however: Chapter cannot tell me to quit my job, divorce my husband or start taking in foster children.

Taking a vow of obedience is certainly a countercultural move in twenty-first century Western culture. But is it incompatible with freedom? I began by questioning our culture's definition of freedom as the absence of constraints on the individual because I believe this is one of our great myths, another of the lies we live with. We all know that it is impossible to go through life without any constraints, or any obligations to others. But even a more limited ideal of personal autonomy is an illusion because, as Bob Dylan sang and the ancients knew, you gotta serve *somebody*. There are plenty of candidates queuing up for mastery over my life, but when I've turned them all down and imagined myself free, I'm left serving my own ego. I've known people like this, especially professionally: they worked so hard to establish a career in which they have a lot of autonomy, but then they spend their lives bitterly resenting how no one appreciates them. They're underpaid, under-recognized, and people don't pay enough attention to their opinions. The ego is a hard master, and only when its mastery is broken can we cease caring about whether anyone appreciates us, and get on with living out our joy.

In the end, we might as well be servants of God, because no one else understands us so well, or has our interests so much at heart, including our own selves. To quote Rowan Williams again, "To submit to God is to be most directly in touch with what is most real. To refuse that submission is not to be free of an alien violence but to become an alien to yourself."[18] And if we're going to give our best service to God, we need to be accountable to others. I know that I'm capable of the most outrageous rationalizations for behavior that would be manifestly unacceptable to anyone else, so I need others to keep me honest. Taking a vow of obedience isn't the only way to get this accountability, of course. But we need to find it somewhere, because the idea that we don't need the insight of others is a lie we can choose to live with, but we'll never live with it alone. It's bound to bring a few more with it, and when we've rejected all authority, who will be left to evict them?

Questions for Reflection

1. Paradox is one of the features of the spiritual life: Jesus said, "For those who want to save their life will lose it, but those who lose their life for my sake will find it," (Matt 16:25). He also said that if we obey his teaching, we will be free (John 8:31–32). Freedom is won through obedience; how have you seen this principle at work in your own life or the lives of others?

2. When have you seen authority abused, and submission to authority becoming destructive? Were there warning signs that could have alerted someone to the problem before it got out of hand? What might have been done in those situations to prevent the abuse of power?

3. Think about the authority relations in your own life, those who have authority over you, and those subject to your authority. Where does the exercise of authority seem to be working well, and where is it not? What makes the difference?

4. Christ turned authority relations upside down: those who would be chief in the Church must be the servant of all, and the last will be first. What are the characteristics of "servant leadership"? What does it mean to serve Christ in the least, last and lowest?

5. Have you ever taken a principled stand against authority? Whose authority was at issue: a boss, clergy member, civil authority, parents? How did you decide to take the position you did? What was the outcome?

Steps into Obedience

1. Make a list of the people in your life whose judgment you trust, whose advice you would follow. Would you say that in some sense you submit to their authority? Why?

2. Experiment with small, hidden acts of obedience. For example, the next time someone asks something of you that you have

every right to refuse, try giving in graciously. Then reflect on the experience: how does it feel to lay your own wishes aside in favor of someone else's? What do you learn from it?

3. Think of the people over whom you have authority: children, students, employees. Look for an opportunity to do something for them that you don't have to do. Reflect on the experience; what does it teach you about "servant leadership"?

4. The Church is a community where everyone gets some of what they want but no one gets everything their way. Look for opportunities to subordinate your will to the interests of the Church community. Perhaps a change in liturgy or a new way of doing parish business has your feathers ruffled. How does it feel to simply accept this and let it go?

5. In what areas of your life are you holding out against God? Perhaps you've turned your house over to him, but you've still got your junk piled up in a few corners. What step toward obedience in one of these areas can you take today?

6. Richard Foster has written extensively on the discipline of submission, or obedience. His book *Celebration of Discipline* and the companion workbook provide an excellent introduction and a tool for thinking about obedience. In another book, *The Challenge of the Disciplined Life: Christian Reflections on Money, Sex and Power*, he goes more deeply into both the creative use and the abuse of spiritual authority. These are extremely helpful resources for anyone concerned about the value and limits of obedience in the church, the family, the workplace and public life.

Prayer

Father, "thy will be done." If we say this enough times, will we mean it? It's a tough one, and even your beloved Son, in whom you were well pleased, struggled with it. Grant us the grace truly to will what you will, and the freedom that comes with relinquishing the need to be in control. Give us grace also to resist courageously when anyone abuses the power you've put into their hands, and does harm to the smallest and lowest—even to us. Amen.

15

JOY
OUR "LITTLE PORTION"

[J]oy is a divine gift, coming from union with God in Christ. It is still there even in times of darkness and difficulty, giving cheerful courage in the face of disappointment, and an inward serenity and confidence through sickness and suffering. Those who possess it can rejoice in weakness, insults, hardship, and persecutions for Christ's sake; for when they are weak, then they are strong.

—*The Principles of the Third Order of the Society
of Saint Francis,* Day Twenty-Nine

THERE'S A STORY ABOUT ST. FRANCIS in which he and Friar Leo were making a winter journey from Perugia to the Porziuncula. The Porziuncula, or "Little Portion," was a small plot of land just below Assisi containing a tiny chapel, which was one of several that Francis restored after his conversion. The chapel and grounds were owned by the Benedictines, who rented it to Francis and his followers for a token payment of fish; the place became the seat of the Franciscan movement and remains its spiritual home. Well into their journey, road-weary and numb with cold, Francis began to conjure up images of fantastic success on the part of the Order, and to maintain that in none of these was perfect joy to be found.

The friars might achieve impressive scholarship, admired by all the world, but this would not bring perfect joy. They might carry out miraculous healings, even raise the dead, but neither would this bring perfect joy. They might convert the last infidel on earth, but perfect joy would not be found here either. Finally, exasperated, Brother Leo begs Francis in the name of God to tell him, where *is* perfect joy? Francis responds with a different set of images: they return to the Porziuncula and the doorkeeper fails to recognize them, takes them for robbers and shuts them out in the cold. There, Francis says, is perfect joy. If they keep knocking, and the doorkeeper comes out and beats them with a club, abuses them and tosses them out into the snow, there, he insists, is perfect joy. "If we shall bear all these things patiently and with cheerfulness, thinking on the suffering of Christ the blessed, which we ought to bear patiently for His love, O Friar Leo, write that here and in this is perfect joy."[1]

My fieldwork complete, I'm finally home after five long months. My brothers and sisters in the St. Clare fellowship received me affectionately, and in any case it's August in Seattle so there's no snow for them to throw me into. The week in Ghana visiting the slave castles was followed by a focus on European atrocity sites, of which there are plenty. I've been to the concentration camps at Auschwitz and Sachsenhausen, seen the headquarters of Nazi and Communist secret police in Budapest where dissidents of every kind were detained and tortured, and a prison in Warsaw where the story was much the same. I've visited various museums of state terror, countless small Jewish museums, each with its own local Holocaust stories, and I've been to Jewish cemeteries where the birth dates vary but most of the deaths are listed as the early 1940s. I've toured the Checkpoint Charlie museum in Berlin, been taken around the Catholic and Protestant neighborhoods of Belfast, and seen an exhibition on the Troubles in Derry, where I missed by a couple of hours a riot involving about a hundred people throwing stones and petrol bombs. I've visited the Museum of Famine in a small town west of Dublin, and seen an exhibition on the Atlantic slave trade in Liverpool. If Francis was right, then with all this horror fresh in my mind, it's as good a time as any to write about joy.

One of the earliest lessons we have to learn as Christians is the distinction between joy and happiness. You can't go too far into the gospels without being forced to see the difference: at the close of the Beatitudes Jesus tells his disciples to "rejoice and be glad" when people insult, abuse and persecute them (Matt 5:11–12). On the night before his execution, knowing what was coming, Jesus tried to prepare his disciples for the ordeal ahead. Then he said, "I have said these thing to you so that my joy may be in you, and that your joy may be complete" (John 15:11). These are pretty strange words coming from a leader who knows his followers have risked everything for him and are about to see him tortured and strung up by the occupying forces, when they'd hoped he would be the one to redeem Israel (Luke 24:21). Happiness is a feeling of satisfaction we have when things are going well for us, and that very night the disciples were going to find things going disastrously wrong: their Messiah turned over to Rome, their high hopes crushed, their movement apparently ended and themselves in serious jeopardy.

But Jesus could speak of joy—his joy and theirs—because his is the "upside-down kingdom,"[2] where the last shall be first, the prostitutes enter heaven before the clergy, and the poor and the meek inherit both heaven and earth. What looked like Jesus' moment of humiliating defeat would be, he knew, his moment of triumph. St. Paul learned this lesson in his own life: "Therefore I am content with weaknesses, insults, hardships, persecutions, and calamities, for the sake of Christ; for whenever I am weak, then I am strong" (2 Cor 12:10). And though Francis weakened his body with fasting and meditated often on the Passion, he would sometime dance down the road, singing in French and playing air violin.[3] What Jesus knew, and what both Paul and Francis learned from him, is that joy is another of those paradoxes of the spiritual life, entirely compatible with danger, failure and sorrow. Unlike happiness, joy has very little to do with our feelings and doesn't depend on external circumstances; in this respect, joy is a lot like peace. At the same time that Jesus promised his disciples joy, he promised them peace (John 14:27), but he was careful to say that this was not peace as the world understood it. This was saying a lot, because what "the world" of that time and place would have understood by *shalom* is much richer than our word "peace," which connotes merely an absence of conflict or anxiety. Shalom is a total state of physical, emotional, social and spiritual well-being, which includes not only safety and security but prosperity, health, wholeness and completion.

Yet Jesus was promising his followers something beyond even that. His peace would be with them, and us, even in the midst of anxiety, peril and suffering: "In the world you face persecution. But take courage; *I have conquered the world*" (John 16:33). The peace of Christ is a peace that "surpasses all understanding" (Phil 4:7); in other words, it is a peace that makes no sense. Or it makes sense only if we look behind the veil of our natural understanding, and into the face of reality as God sees it: the world conquered by Christ, death overcome, Israel—and all humanity—redeemed beyond anything the disciples had imagined. Peace, then, is not the absence of conflict but the assurance that we belong to the God who loved us "to the uttermost,"[4] and nothing and no one can touch us without his permission. In the same way, the joy Christ gives us is far deeper than our circumstances and has little to do with how we feel about them. Unlike happiness, joy is less a feeling than a settled conviction, not spiritual goose bumps but the certain knowledge that, as Lady Julian of Norwich put it, "all will be well, and all will be well, and all manner of thing will be well."[5] Or, as Archbishop Desmond Tutu likes to reassure people, "I've read the end of the book—we win!"

It *is* reassuring. Likewise, to know that whatever sufferings I may endure for the cause of Christ are precious to him and not forgotten makes them a joy rather than a burden. And to know that when suffering comes my way, not because of Christ but just because the world is a hard place, he is with me in them—that, too, is a great comfort. I've learned that I can have joy in the face of disappointment and failure, sickness and loss in my own life. As I said, this is one of the elementary lessons of the faith. What I find harder to understand, though, is how I can have joy in spite of the suffering of others. The weeks I spent touring atrocity museums made this question both more clear and more urgent than usual. I saw video footage of the trial of seventeen Auschwitz administrators, one of whom "beat men's testicles until they died." I read the memoirs of a prisoner who served as Dr. Mengele's assistant,[6] who describes the gruesome medical experiments carried out on camp prisoners, including children, even infants. In one case, the corpses of a father and son were being boiled to reduce them more efficiently to skeletons. When the cauldron was momentarily left unattended, starving prisoners stole pieces of flesh off the bones and ate them: "When [they] discovered what they had been eating they were transfixed, paralysed with terror."[7] In Budapest I heard the testimony of Abbot Vendel Endredy, arrested in 1950 and tortured by the Communist regime: he was interrogated for eighteen hours, given electric shocks, forced to stand on tiptoe on a plank studded with nails and flanked by red-hot plates until he collapsed. He was placed in a tiny underground cell under a dripping sewer pipe, where he couldn't lie down for two weeks, nor lean against the wall when he sat. "My primary prayer in those ghastly days was: Would that I could meet my Maker, lest I hurt someone with my confession."[8]

I saw Abbot Endredy's cell, and others specially designed to keep prisoners waist-deep in water, to keep them from sitting or lying down, to cut off the air supply, to administer shocks and beatings. I've seen hooks on which prisoners, arms bound behind their backs, were suspended from the wrists so as to pull the shoulders out of joint. I've stood in a gas chamber and stared straight into the ovens, and I've looked into the faces of old men and women riddled with survivor's guilt. With all this suffering before me, the idea of joy seems almost indecent, an insult to the memory of every victim whose story I've heard, and the many more whose stories I haven't heard. Still, when Christ was about to enter into all of the suffering of humankind, he spoke of his joy, and ours. How is this possible?

I'm not sure. I'm still pretty overwhelmed by the magnitude of the atrocities I've seen, and by the question of my own complicity in them. If I haven't actually protested the genocide occurring in Sudan, I'm forced to see myself in the Germans who failed to stand against the Nazis. But even if I have, it's hard to see how I can have joy while conscious of the suffering of others. And yet, I know that there is no genuine joy *without* the consciousness of others' pain; such "joy" would be mere escapism. I can choose to ignore human misery—or indeed, animal misery—and have happiness, since happiness only implies satisfaction with how things are going for me. But joy, as the *Principles* remind us, is a divine gift, "coming from union with God in Christ." If I am one with Christ, then in the spirit of *compassio* I enter into the suffering of others, as he does. The morning I went to Auschwitz, I arrived a half-hour early to the bus stop in Krakow, so I had a little time on my hands and decided to explore the neighborhood. I turned into a small street that had a convent on one side, and a garden on the other. Opening the iron gate, I discovered that the garden contained the most beautiful Stations of the Cross that I've ever seen.[9] I have to agree with a friend who said that sometimes God is not subtle. In every story of every victim that I heard that day, I saw Christ falling under the weight of the cross, and knew that he had chosen to be present with each one of them, to share in their anguish. And if I am one with him, I will find some way to do the same.

But where does joy come into this? The day I visited the Topography of Terror Museum in Berlin, which occupies the site of the former SS headquarters, I wrote the following to a friend:

> The only way I can see to have joy in spite of all this is because God is both willing and able to bring justice and healing—complete justice, and complete healing. I trust this, in practice. But I can see it coming across as a facile dismissal of real suffering—

"Oh, it's no big deal, God will make it all come out in the wash." God as detergent.

But despite the very real danger of descending into a callous complacency, I believe that the answer does lie in Lady Julian's conviction that "all manner of thing will be well." Tom Wright likes to point out that while Jesus healed numerous people during his earthly ministry, if his objective was merely to heal as many as possible, he didn't do very well.[10] It was, after all, a pretty short-lived career, and there were always other things to do, like telling stories and aggravating the Pharisees. But the point wasn't the numbers; rather, Jesus was showing us what happens when he touches people—even with dirt and spit (John 9:6). Human brokenness *is* a big deal—big enough for God to assume human flesh and take the whole weight of that brokenness on himself. But when he did so, he made possible the full, complete healing of all our wounds, even the deepest wounds of the soul. What Francis was trying to tell Leo on the way to the Porziuncula is that it is here, in this knowledge, and nowhere else, that perfect joy is to be found.

The Porziuncula. The name of the chapel is actually Santa Maria degli Angeli, but it's taken on the name of the land on which it was built. In the sixteenth century a large church was erected over the chapel, to protect it from the elements and to accommodate the large number of pilgrims who come to see the place Francis called the *caput et mater* (head and mother) of his Order. The chapel is tiny, simple and heartbreakingly beautiful, and as I stand in the doorway running my hand over the rough stone, I feel a profound sense of coming home.

It's a rare moment of peace on this, my second visit to Assisi. I scheduled a week alone here, to help make the transition from vacationing with my family to facing the atrocity sites of Eastern Europe. On my first visit ten months before, the place had charmed and delighted me, and I looked forward eagerly to a longer stay and the opportunity to see more of the sites associated with Francis' life. On the train in from Venice, I felt a strong sense of purpose to my visit, that there was a specific reason for my being here. "Oh cool," I thought, "this'll be great." But it soon became apparent that this visit wasn't going to charm and delight me—it was going to challenge me, and the challenge started right away. I walked a couple blocks from my hotel to the bishop's residence, where the famous scene took place in which Francis shed his clothes, returned them to his father, and announced that he would from henceforth acknowledge only his Father in heaven. I peered through the gates into the courtyard where this renunciation occurred, and expected to enjoy mentally conjuring up the scene, but was brought up short. It dawned on me that what I was looking at was the Cross: Francis' cross, the grief he had to endure when following Christ cost him an important relationship.

And so it went: the rugged little hermitages where Francis withdrew to be alone with God, the island where he spent an entire Lent fasting, the places where he washed the sores of lepers, all of them spoke loudly of Francis' single-minded commitment, and raised uncomfortable questions about my own. Francis' devotion to Lady Poverty, for instance—how seriously was I willing to take this whole simplicity thing? What would it mean to take it as seriously as Francis did? The point of the Third Order, and indeed of all Franciscan Orders, is not to relive Francis' life, but to live our own with the same goal and the same dedication as he lived his. I've spent years examining my consumption patterns and making modest changes, but Francis was willing to embrace radical change. Am I? Before he adopted the habit, Francis once changed clothes with a beggar. Can I honestly see myself doing that?—or even just giving her my coat, when I have plenty more at home? At least I can say, looking down once again at the rough rock bed on which Francis slept, that I've learned to enjoy praying through the wakeful periods at night, but I suspect it's a lot easier on a feather bed with a down pillow.

The whole week in Assisi I was haunted by these questions, and by the sense that God brought me here to take a hard look at my life and values, what is negotiable and what is not. On the train heading south to Rome, where I'd catch my flight to Budapest, I felt the issue was settled, at least for now, and a peace and joy descended on me that has not left me. I expect I'll have to go through this process many times, as my growth gets shaggy and the vinedresser has to prune me back (John 15:1–2). When that happens, I'll be able to look back on those peaceful moments in the Porziuncula where I knew that, whatever costs it may exact from me, this is my spiritual home. I belong to this place, and it belongs to me. That was how Francis felt about it: when he lay dying at the bishop's palace, he asked to be brought here, stripped and laid on the ground in the place he loved best. Surrounded by his brothers, he told them: "I have done what was my duty to do—may Christ show you what is yours." On my first trip to Assisi, with my sister driving and me navigating, we noticed that it really does seem that all roads lead to Rome. "But some roads lead to Assisi," she said. This is where my road has taken me; may Christ show you yours.

Questions for Reflection

1. Francis believed that joy was the safest remedy against temptation: "The devils cannot harm the servant of Christ when they see he is filled with holy joy."[11] How do you think joy might protect us from evil?

2. Was there ever a time in your life when you knew joy in the midst of turmoil or suffering? How did you take hold of that joy in spite of your external circumstances?

3. The people of God are meant to live in joy, but we often don't. What are some of the factors that keep from holding onto our joy? Many of these are undoubtedly personal, but are there social and cultural forces that interfere with our joy?

4. Joy is not primarily a matter of feelings; nevertheless, most of us have felt it at some time. Are there places or occasions where you find it easier to be joyful? People who bring you into joy?

Steps into Joy

1. Make a list of all the reasons you can think of to be joyful, in spite of whatever is going on in your life. Put the list someplace where you can re-read it often.

2. Joy is partly a product of gratitude. Thank God for every item on your list of reasons to be joyful. Someone has suggested imagining that the only things in our lives we get to keep are the things we thank God for. Try starting that prayer of thanksgiving, and see how long it goes.

3. Cultivate the art of celebration. You don't have to wait for a wedding, a graduation or even a birthday. Maybe it's the first day in a week that your kid didn't get bullied, or you finally got the dog's vaccinations up to date, or met a deadline at work. Do something a little special to celebrate, and in the midst of your celebration, take a moment to remember those who suffer.

4. If there's a special place that brings you back to joy, how can you spend a little more time there? If it's far away, can you plan a trip there? If it's local, can you work little visits into your schedule on a more regular basis?

5. Keep your eyes on the goal. When your life breaks over you and you feel yourself going under, think about your death, and meeting Jesus face to face. What will be important to you then? Do you think the things that are eating at you now will fade into the background then? Then let them fade now. You may not be able to forget them entirely, but let them assume their true proportions.

Prayer

FRANCIS: A SONG FOR THE ROAD

Lord, you are all my joy.
You are all my love,
   all my passion,
   all my strength.
You are all my pleasure,
   all my delight.
You are all my fire,
   all my life.
All my sweetness,
   all my madness,
   all my longing,
   my bitter emptiness,
   my sweet satisfaction,
   my ecstasy, and my peace.
You are all, and all, and all
   to me.

16

A BRIEF BIOGRAPHY OF ST. FRANCIS

FRANCIS OF ASSISI WAS BORN IN 1181 OR 1182 to Pietro Bernardone, a wealthy cloth merchant, and his French wife Lady Pica. Pietro was away trading in France when his son was born, and the child was christened Giovanni, but his father changed it to "Francesco" (the little Frenchman) on his return. Pietro had an affection for all things French, which Francis himself came to share: at his most joyful, he liked to improvise love songs in French and sing them to God. Francis was not much of a student, however, nor did he have any great enthusiasm for taking up his father's business.

In his youth Francis had a reputation as a playboy and a *bon vivant*, treating his friends to good times at his father's expense, though he was equally generous with the poor. He dreamed of distinguishing himself in battle, but at about age twenty he was taken prisoner in Perugia, and languished there ill for a year before being ransomed by his father. His convalescence back in Assisi was marked by uncertainty about his future, but eventually he made another attempt at a military career. This one ended when a dream turned him back to Assisi, and he withdrew from his former pleasures, embracing beggars and lepers and spending much of his time wandering the countryside in search of direction. He finally found it at a little half-ruined church called San Damiano. Francis was kneeling before its Byzantine cross one day when suddenly the

Lord spoke to him from it: "Francis, go and repair my house, which as you can see, is falling into ruins." Francis took this command literally at first, and restored several derelict churches in the area before coming to understand that it was not churches he was meant to rebuild, but the Church itself.

The changes in Francis' life made him appear increasingly eccentric in the eyes of the citizens of Assisi. Relations with his father became more and more strained until eventually, humiliated and fed up, Pietro hauled his son before the Bishop of Assisi and demanded that he renounce his inheritance. Francis, in a gesture that has resonated through the centuries, took off his clothes before the bishop and assembled people. Handing what remained of his possessions to Pietro, Francis said, "Until now I have called you my father on earth, but from now on I desire to say only, 'Our Father who art in Heaven.'" The bishop took Francis under his care, and soon Francis was himself receiving followers, who joined him in renouncing worldly goods and nursing lepers, restoring churches and performing works of charity. Dressed in the clothing of beggars, Francis and his companions set out without money or supplies to preach repentance and the kingdom of God. The brothers took shelter where they could, and offered manual labor in exchange for food, but when work could not be found they accepted alms. The hunger, cold, sickness and the general physical misery they experienced were forgotten under the spell of Francis' charm. Their radical attempt to live the gospel initially made them objects of derision, but in time the scorn turned to respect and even veneration.

The movement grew rapidly: within ten years of having their Rule accepted by the pope, they were able to draw some 5,000 friars and a further 500 aspirants to a Chapter held outside Assisi. The movement was widening as well. In 1212 Francis had received the vows of the eighteen-year-old Clare, who went on to found the Second Franciscan Order of Poor Ladies, known after her death as the Poor Clares. In 1221, the Rule of the Order of Penance or "Third Order" was accepted by the pope, opening the way for still greater growth by making room for people from all walks of life. Francis continued to travel around Italy exhorting the people, and ultimately traveled as far as Egypt where he preached the Christian faith to Sultan Malek Kemel. But by the time he returned to Italy, already infected with the trachoma that would leave him nearly blind, his Order was in disarray. Growth was making it increasingly difficult to remain true to the original vision of gospel simplicity, and the attempt to inject a bit of realism and prudence into the organization looked to Francis like compromise and betrayal. He resigned his head-ship of the Order and spent the remainder of his life trying to lead by example alone.

Like Christ himself, Francis alternated periods of preaching with times of seclusion and intense prayer. Two years before his death, he retired to Monte Alverna for forty days of prayer and fasting. Passing his time in solitude and meditation on the Passion of Christ, he asked two favors of the Lord: that he would know both the pain Jesus had experienced in his Passion, and the love that had compelled him to go through with it. This prayer was dramatically answered when Francis received the Stigmata: the five wounds of Christ's crucifixion impressed in his own flesh. His body already frail from poverty and self-denial, his eyes burning from trachoma, the Stigmata added to Francis' suffering. Yet he returned to Assisi and paid a visit to St. Clare at San Damiano where, in anguish and virtually blind, he dictated his magnificent hymn of praise, the *Canticle of the Creatures*. Less than a year later, Francis lay dying at the bishop's palace in Assisi. When the end was close, he asked to be taken back to the Porziuncula, the little chapel and settlement that was the cradle of his Order. There, faithful to Lady Poverty to the end, he lay naked on the ground surrounded by his brothers, and gave them his final exhortation: "I have done what was my duty to do—may Christ show you what is yours." He was taken at last by "Sister Death," whose praise he had sung in a verse added to the *Canticle of the Creatures* just before his death on October 3, 1226, at age forty-five. Francis was canonized by Pope Gregory IX in 1228, and his feast day is cele-brated October 4th.

THE CANTICLE OF THE CREATURES

Most High, all powerful, good Lord, to you be praise, glory, honor
and all blessing.

Only to you, Most High, do they belong and no one is worthy to
call upon your name.

May you be praised, my Lord, with all your creatures, especially
brother sun, through whom you lighten the day for us.

He is beautiful and radiant with great splendor, and he signifies you,
O Most High.

Be praised, my Lord, for sister moon and the stars: Clear and
precious and lovely, they are formed in heaven.

Be praised, my Lord, for brother wind and by air and clouds,
clear skies and all weathers, by which you give sustenance to
your creatures.

Be praised, my Lord, for sister water, who is very useful and humble
and precious and pure.

Be praised, my Lord, for brother fire, by whom the night is
illumined for us: he is beautiful and cheerful, full of power
and strength.

Be praised, my Lord, for sister, our mother earth, who sustains
and governs us and produces diverse fruits and colored flowers
and grass.

Be praised, my Lord, by all those who forgive for love of you and
who bear weakness and tribulation.

Blessed are those who endure in peace: For by you Most High, they
will be crowned.

Be praised, my Lord, for our sister, the death of the body, from
whom no one living is able to flee; woe to those who are dying
in mortal sin.

Blessed are those who are found doing your most holy will, for the
second death will do them no harm.

Praise and bless my Lord and give him thanks and serve him with
great humility.

RESOURCES

For information on the Third Order of the Society of St. Francis, please see the Order's website: www.tssf.org. This site contains links to other Franciscan Orders, including the Roman Catholic Secular Franciscan Order and the Order of Ecumenical Franciscans, as well as Anglican branches of the Third Order in other parts of the world. Alternatively, write to:

> The Inquirer's Secretary
> Little Portion Friary
> P.O. Box 399
> Mt. Sinai, NY 11766

Information about other Anglican orders open to lay people can be found at: http://anglicansonline.org/resources/orders.html. For links to Roman Catholic Third Orders in the Carmelite, Dominican, Benedictine and other traditions, see: http://www.memorare.com/reform/third.html. An extensive list of Anglican, Roman Catholic and ecumenical orders can be found at: http://www.rosmini.org/order/.

The Society of St. Francis, like many religious communities, also offers the option of becoming an associate. This is a way of following Francis by affiliating with all the Franciscan Orders, but without taking formal vows in any of them. The resources listed above provide information on this option in the orders where it is available.

ENDNOTES

PREFACE

1. It should be noted that some bodies prefer not to use the term "Third Order," feeling that it implies a lesser status than that associated with the First and Second Orders (active friars and sisters, and contemplative nuns, respectively). In the Roman Catholic Church, for example, our counterpart is known as the "Secular Franciscan Order."

2. See, e.g., Murray Bodo, *Francis: The Journey and the Dream* (Cincinnati: St. Anthony Messenger, 1988); Murray Bodo, *The Way of St. Francis: The Challenge of Franciscan Spirituality for Everyone* (Cincinnati: St. Anthony Messenger, 1995); Marie Dennis, Joseph Nangle, Cynthia Moe-Lobeda and Stuart Taylor, *St. Francis and the Foolishness of God* (Maryknoll, NY: Orbis, 2000); William Short, *Poverty and Joy: The Franciscan Tradition* (Maryknoll, NY: Orbis, 1999); John Michael Talbot, with Steve Rabey, *The Lessons of St. Francis: How to Bring Simplicity and Spirituality into Your Daily Life* (New York: Plume, 1997).

3. For official information on the Third Order of the Society of Saint Francis, including links to other Franciscan Orders and information for inquirers, see: www.tssf.org. Links to other Anglican orders open to lay people can be found at: http://anglicansonline.org/resources/orders.html. For links to Roman Catholic Third Orders in the Carmelite, Dominican, Benedictine and other traditions, see: http://www.memorare.com/reform/third.html. Links to Anglican, Roman Catholic and ecumenical orders can be found at: http://www.rosmini.org/order/.

CHAPTER 1

1. John Michael Talbot, with Steve Rabey, *The Lessons of St. Francis: How to Bring Simplicity and Spirituality into Your Daily Life* (New York: Plume, 1997), 24.

2. All Scripture references are from the New Revised Standard Version, unless otherwise noted.

3. Thomas Keating, *Open Mind, Open Heart: The Contemplative Dimension of the Gospel* (New York: Continuum, 1997), 76.

4. My intention here is emphatically *not* to imply that centering prayer isn't a worthwhile practice; many people have found it immensely helpful. I am only objecting to the rigidity and dogmatism I've seen attached to it

among certain teachers, and these problems can be associated with any method of prayer, including the ones I practice myself.

5. Teresa of Avila, *Interior Castle* (New York: Doubleday, 1961, trans. E. Allison Peers).

CHAPTER 2

1. *The Principles of the Third Order of the Society of Saint Francis* arrange the Rule into short sections so that one may be read each day of the month.

2. Teresa of Avila, *Interior Castle*, 135–36.

3. Rosemary Haughton, *The Passionate God* (New York: Paulist, 1981).

4. Ibid., 51.

5. *The Admonitions* I, in *St. Francis of Assisi: Omnibus of Sources* (Quincy, IL: Franciscan Press, 1991, ed. Marion A. Habig), 78–79.

6. *Letter to a General Chapter*, in *St. Francis of Assisi: Omnibus of Sources*, 103–8.

7. Ibid, 105–6.

8. Quoted in *Christianity Today*, April 2004, Vol. 48, No. 4, 31.

CHAPTER 3

1. *The Principles of the Third Order of the Society of Saint Francis*, Days Fourteen and Sixteen.

2. William J. Short, OFM, *Poverty and Joy: The Franciscan Tradition* (Maryknoll, NY: Orbis, 1999); John Michael Talbot, *The Lessons of St. Francis*.

3. Short, *Poverty and Joy*, ch. 5.

4. St. Bonaventure, *Major Life of St. Francis*, X.1, in *St. Francis of Assisi: Omnibus of Sources*, 705–6.

5. Marie Dennis, Joseph Nangle OFM, Cynthia Moe-Lobeda and Stuart Taylor, *St. Francis and the Foolishness of God* (Maryknoll, NY: Orbis, 1993).

6. See Ronald M. Mrozinski, OFM, *The Franciscan Active-Contemplative Synthesis and the Role of Centers of Prayer* (Chicago: Franciscan Herald Press, 1981); also Third Order American Province, Society of St. Francis, *Forming the Soul of a Franciscan*, 2000, ch. 22A, "The Contemplative within the Franciscan Vocation."

7. See the excellent short summary of the history and contemporary significance of the Daily Office offered by the Church of the Good Shepherd, Rosemont, on their website: http://orthodoxanglican.org/asb/office.html.

8. Other "little Offices" include noonday prayer and compline, recited at the close of the day.

9. From "The Praises," to be said before the Office; quoted in William J. Short, *Poverty and Joy*, 83.

10. *The Ecstasy of St. Francis*, at L'Eremo delle Carceri.

11. Ugolino di Monte Santa Maria, *The Little Flowers of Saint Francis* (New York: Vintage, 1998, trans. W. Heywood).

12. Short, *Poverty and Joy*, 84–85.

13. The Eucharistic Meditations of the Curé d'Ars, "Visit to the Blessed Sacrament—a method of making it," Meditation 22, www.carmelites.ie/Archive/euchmed2.htm#Med%2022.

14. Charles Williams, *The Greater Trumps* (London: Regent, 2003 [1932]), 16.

15. My all-time favorite is *The Gospel of John* starring Henry Ian Cusick as Jesus, released in 2003 by Visual Bible International.

16. Richard Foster, *Celebration of Discipline: The Path to Spiritual Growth* (San Francisco: Harper, 1978).

17. Teresa of Avila, *Interior Castle*; Evelyn Underhill, *Practical Mysticism: A Little Book for Normal People* (London: Dent, 1914).

18. Keating, *Open Mind, Open Heart*, 11.

19. Many of these mystics' writings are helpfully summarized in Dorothee Soelle, *The Silent Cry: Mysticism and Resistance* (Minneapolis: Fortress, 2001, trans. Barbara and Martin Rumscheidt). See also Saskia Murk-Jansen, *Brides in the Desert: The Spirituality of the Beguines* (London: Darton, Longman and Todd, 1998), and Elizabeth A. Dreyer, *Passionate Spirituality: Hildegard of Bingen and Hadewijch of Brabant* (Mahwah, NJ: Paulist Press, 2005).

20. Talbot, *The Lessons of St. Francis*, 234.

21. 2 Corinthians 11:14.

22. Matthew 7:20.

23. Wolfgang von Goethe, *The Holy Longing*, translated by Robert Bly and quoted in Ronald Rolheiser, *The Holy Longing: The Search for a Christian Spirituality* (New York: Doubleday), 1.

CHAPTER 4

1. Martin Hughes, *Rome: Condensed*, 2nd ed. (Footscray, Australia: Lonely Planet Publications, 2003).

2. Soelle, *The Silent Cry*, 114.

3. Talbot, *The Lessons of St. Francis*, 230.

4. Soelle, *The Silent Cry*, 113–14.

5. Haughton, *The Passionate God*, 14. Obviously, there are many other ways to think about the love of God for us, and one of the most beloved is of God as a parent. Parental imagery brings to the fore other aspects of God's love: its self-giving nature, its unconditional quality. This also furnishes us with a powerful language of love. I chose to write about nuptial imagery, however, because it is much less familiar to most Christians.

6. Quoted in Soelle, *The Silent Cry*, 117.

7. Omer Englebert, *St. Francis of Assisi: A Biography* (Servant Ministries 1979 [1965]), 72.

8. *Legend of the Three Companions* III.7, *St. Francis of Assisi: Omnibus of Sources*, 896–97.

9. Jacopone da Todi, *The Lauds* (New York: Paulist, 1982, trans. Serge and Elizabeth Hughes), 264.

10. Rolheiser, *The Holy Longing*.

11. Dorothee Soelle, *Mysticism and Resistance* (Minneapolis: Augsburg Fortress, 2001), ch. 7.

12. Talbot, *The Lessons of St. Francis*, 123.

13. Haughton, *The Passionate God*, 7.

14. Dorothy L. Sayers makes this point beautifully in her essay, "The Six Other Deadly Sins," ch. 7 in Dorothy L. Sayers, *Creed or Chaos? and Other Essays in Popular Theology* (Manchester, NH: Sophia, 1974 [1947]).

15. Soelle, *The Silent Cry*, 118.

16. St. Francis, *Rule of 1221* XXIII, in *St. Francis of Assisi: Omnibus of Sources*, 51–52.

17. Murray Bodo, *The Way of St. Francis* (Cincinnati: St. Anthony Messenger Press, 1995), 67.

18. The Beguines were a movement that began in the thirteenth century in which (mostly) women lived lives consecrated to God without following a particular rule and, crucially, without the protection of a recognized Order. They include Mechtilde of Magdeburg, Hadewych, Marguerite Por'te and Beatrijs of Nazareth, among others, and they produced some of the greatest mystical texts ever written. They often had close relationships to the established Orders, including the Franciscans, with whom they had much in common. See Saskia Murk-Jansen, *Brides in the Desert: The Spirituality of the Beguines* (London: Darton, Longman and Todd, 1998).

19. Murk-Jansen, *Brides in the Desert*, 13.

20. Emily Zum Brunn, Georgette Epiney-Burgard, and Sheila Hughes, *Women Mystics in Medieval Europe* (St. Paul, MN: Paragon House, 1989), x.

21. Bodo, *The Way of St. Francis*, 56, original emphasis.

22. Talbot, *The Lessons of St. Francis*, 8.

23. Dorothy L. Sayers, *Gaudy Night* (New York: Harper & Row, 1964), 360. Sayers wrote this poem about Oxford, but as a devout Christian, would presumably not object to the present application.

CHAPTER 5

1. Available at www.tssf.org.

2. Thomas of Celano, *The Second Life of St. Francis* XIV.21, in *St. Francis of Assisi: Omnibus of Sources*, 380.

3. St. Bonaventure, *Major Life of St. Francis* V.1, in *St. Francis of Assisi: Omnibus of Sources*, 663.

4. *The Little Flowers of St. Francis of Assisi*, 42.

5. Short, *Poverty and Joy*, 104.

6. Wendy Wright, *Sacred Heart: Gateway to God* (Maryknoll, NY: Orbis, 2001).

7. Soelle, *The Silent Cry*, 139.

8. Ibid., 143.

9. Ibid., 140.

10. *The Principles of the Third Order of the Society of St. Francis*, Day Sixteen.

11. *The Little Flowers of St. Francis of Assisi*, ch. 21.

CHAPTER 6

1. Cf. *The Little Flowers of St. Francis of Assisi*, in *St. Francis of Assisi: Omnibus of Sources*, 1146.
2. *The Little Flowers of St. Francis of Assisi*, ch. 9.
3. *Mirror of Perfection*, in *St. Francis of Assisi: Omnibus of Sources*, 1169–70.
4. Thomas of Celano, *Second Life*, in *St. Francis of Assisi: Omnibus of Sources*, 471.
5. Ibid., 477.
6. *Legend of Perugia*, in *St. Francis of Assisi: Omnibus of Sources*, 999.
7. Foster, *Celebration of Discipline*, 116.
8. Bonaventure, *Major Life*, in *St. Francis of Assisi: Omnibus of Sources*, 671.
9. Rowan Williams, *Teresa of Avila* (London: Continuum, 2004).
10. The Book of Common Prayer (1979) Eucharistic Prayer A.
11. *Mirror of Perfection*, in *St. Francis Of Assisi: Omnibus of Sources*, 1170.
12. Foster, *Celebration of Discipline*.

CHAPTER 7

1. Kathleen Norris, *The Cloister Walk* (NY: Riverhead, 1997).
2. *The Little Flowers of St. Francis of Assisi*, ch. 7.
3. What was historically called "leprosy" is in reality a complex array of diseases, differing greatly in their contagiousness, symptoms and severity.
4. Neil Postman, *Amusing Ourselves to Death* (New York: Penguin, 1985).
5. The Sufi poet Rumi, quoted in Soelle, *The Silent Cry*, 29–30.
6. Talbot, *The Lessons of St. Francis*, 78–79.
7. Thomas of Celano, *Second Life*, in *St. Francis of Assisi: Omnibus of Sources*, 481–82.
8. My "title prohibition" isn't absolute, however: I do use my title when not doing so will create confusion in the workplace, as on official documents. I also use it when I'm advocating for others, in the hope that it will add a little weight on *their* behalf.
9. Erving Goffman, *The Presentation of Self in Everyday Life* (New York: Anchor, 1959).
10. Foster, *Celebration of Discipline*, 89.
11. Ibid.
12. Judith Dean, *Every Pilgrim's Guide to Assisi* (Norwich, UK: Canterbury Press, 2002), 53.
13. *The Little Flowers of St. Francis of Assisi*, in *St. Francis of Assisi: Omnibus of Sources*, 1362.
14. Soelle, *The Silent Cry*.

CHAPTER 8

1. *Second Life*, in *St. Francis of Assisi: Omnibus of Sources*, 411.
2. *The Little Flowers of St. Francis of Assisi*, in *St. Francis of Assisi: Omnibus of Sources*, 434–35.

3. *The Little Flowers of St. Francis of Assisi*, in *St. Francis of Assisi: Omnibus of Sources*, 1327–28.

4. St. Francis, *First Rule of the Third Order*, in *St. Francis of Assisi: Omnibus of Sources*, 169.

5. Dennis et al., *St. Francis and the Foolishness of God*, 9–10.

6. Norris, *The Cloister Walk*, 34.

7. York William Bradshaw and Michael Wallace, *Global Inequalities* (Thousand Oaks, Calif.: Pine Forge, 1996), 15.

8. Ibid.

9. Bonaventure, *Major Life*, in *St. Francis of Assisi: Omnibus of Sources*, 691.

10. Ibid.

11. Christian Feldman, *God's Gentle Rebels: Great Saints of Christianity* (New York: Crossroad, 1995, trans. Peter Heinegg), 103.

12. Ibid., 104.

13. *The Legend of the Three Companions*, in *St. Francis of Assisi: Omnibus of Sources*, 921.

14. C. Wright Mills, *The Sociological Imagination* (New York: Oxford, 1959), 1.

15. Thomas Kelly, *A Testament of Devotion* (San Francisco: Harper SanFrancisco, 1992 [1941]), 91.

16. Foster, *Celebration of Discipline*.

FRANCISCAN ROAD TRIP—GHANA: RADICAL OPENNESS AND REDEMPTION

1. I don't know how many Franciscans use Rite I, with its charmingly archaic language, for the Daily Office. I have the impression that most prefer the contemporary language of Rite II, but I admit to being a bit of a reactionary when it comes to language. I was weaned on the English of the King James Version of the Bible, and to me it's comparable to a perfectly intelligible "dialect" of English.

CHAPTER 9

1. Placid Hermann, OFM. "Introduction to the Writings of St. Francis," in *St. Francis of Assisi: Omnibus of Sources*, 16–18.

2. Talbot, *The Lessons of St. Francis*, 229.

3. *Legend of Perugia*, in *St. Francis of Assisi: Omnibus of Sources*, 1049.

4. Ibid., 208

5. Thomas of Celano, *Second Life*, in *St. Francis of Assisi: Omnibus of Sources*, 517–19.

6. Ibid., 216

7. Ibid., 72.

8. Englebert, *St. Francis of Assisi: A Biography*, 136.

9. Rowan Williams, *Silence and Honey Cakes* (Oxford: Lion Hudson Place, 2004), 113.

10. See e.g. the anonymous fourteenth-century work *The Cloud of Unknowing* (Mahwah, NJ: Paulist, 1982, ed. James Walsh).

CHAPTER 10

1. The three aims are to make Christ known, to spread the spirit of love and harmony, and to live simply.

2. *Forming the Soul of a Franciscan*, Third Order, American Province, Society of St. Francis, 2000, 76.

3. Thomas of Celano, *Second Life*, in *St. Francis of Assisi: Omnibus of Sources*, 426.

4. See Kathleen Norris, *Amazing Grace: A Vocabulary of Faith* (New York: Riverhead, 1998), for other scary churchy words.

5. Bonaventure, *Major Life*, in *St. Francis of Assisi: Omnibus of Sources*, 637.

6. Englebert, *St. Francis of Assisi: A Biography*, 33.

7. Many postulants and novices complete the formation process by mail rather than through a formation class.

8. The most helpful thing I have found to interpret *Interior Castle* is the chapter by the same name in Rowan Williams, *Teresa of Avila* (London: Continuum, 1991).

9. Dianne Aid, convener of the St. Clare Fellowship in Seattle, WA.

CHAPTER 11

1. Talbot, *The Lessons of St. Francis*, 232–33.

2. Thomas of Celano, *First Life*, in *St. Francis of Assisi: Omnibus of Sources*, 288–89.

3. *The Little Flowers of St. Francis of Assisi*, in *St. Francis of Assisi: Omnibus of Sources*, 1436–41.

4. Third Order Chapter, 1999, quoted in *Forming the Soul of a Franciscan*, 2000, Third Order of the Society of St. Francis.

5. *The Testament of St. Francis*, in *St. Francis of Assisi: Omnibus of Sources*, 67.

CHAPTER 12

1. This question comes from the profession liturgy of the Third Order.

2. The information on the formation process is taken from the Third Order's webpage, "Formation of a Tertiary," http://www.tssf.org/form.htm.

CHAPTER 13

1. St. Francis of Assisi, *The Rule of 1221*, St. Francis of Assisi, *The Rule of 1223*, in *St. Francis of Assisi: Omnibus of Sources*, 42; original italics.

2. Celano, *Second Life*, in *St. Francis of Assisi: Omnibus of Sources*, 456–57.

3. *Legend of Perugia*, in *St. Francis of Assisi: Omnibus of Sources*, 1058–59; emphasis added.

4. Murray Bodo has written some delicate meditations on Clare's feelings for Francis in *Clare: A Light in the Garden* (Cincinnati: St. Anthony Messenger Press, 1979).

5. Celano, *Second Life*, in *St. Francis of Assisi: Omnibus of Sources*, 527.

6. Norris, *The Cloister Walk*.

7. Celano, *Second Life*, in *St. Francis of Assisi: Omnibus of Sources*, 493.

8. Philippians 2:6.

CHAPTER 14

1. Orlando Patterson, *Slavery and Social Death* (Cambridge: Harvard University Press, 1982).

2. Bonaventure, *Major Life*, in *St. Francis of Assisi: Omnibus of Sources*, 673–74.

3. Ibid., 674.

4. Quoted in Englebert, *St. Francis of Assisi: A Biography*, 262.

5. Ibid., 264.

6. C.S. Lewis, *The World's Last Night, and Other Essays* (San Diego: Harvest Books, 1988), ch. 3.

7. For a useful discussion of submission, see Richard Foster, *Celebration of Discipline*. Foster provides a more extensive discussion of the use and abuse of spiritual authority in *The Challenge of the Disciplined Life: Christian Reflections on Money, Sex and Power* (San Francisco: Harper, 1989).

8. Celano, *Second Life*, in *St. Francis of Assisi: Omnibus of Sources*, 476.

9. The 2004 Mere Sermon, delivered on April 20th at St. Benet's Church, Cambridge, UK. For the full text, see: http://www.archbishopof canterbury.org/sermons_speeches/040420.html.

10. *The Little Flowers of St. Francis of Assisi*, in *St. Francis of Assisi: Omnibus of Sources*, 1323–24.

11. Ibid., 1375–77.

12. St. Francis of Assisi, *Letter to a Minister*, in *St. Francis of Assisi: Omnibus of Sources*, 110.

13. St. Francis of Assisi, *The Rule of 1223*, in *St. Francis of Assisi: Omnibus of Sources*, 63.

14. St. Francis of Assisi, *The Admonitions*, in *St. Francis of Assisi: Omnibus of Sources*, 78–80.

15. St. Francis of Assisi, *The Rule of 1221*, in *St. Francis of Assisi: Omnibus of Sources*, 35.

16. A Tertiary's spiritual director, if a priest, may or may not be their confessor as well; it is at the individual's discretion.

17. St. Francis of Assisi, *Letter to a General Chapter*, in *St. Francis of Assisi: Omnibus of Sources*, 107.

18. The 2004 Mere Sermon, delivered on April 20th at St. Benet's Church, Cambridge, UK.

CHAPTER 15

1. *The Little Flowers of St. Francis of Assisi*, ch. 8.
2. Donald B. Kraybill, *The Upside-Down Kingdom*, 2nd ed. (Scottdale, Penn.: Herald Press, 1990).
3. Celano, *Second Life*, in *St. Francis of Assisi: Omnibus of Sources*, 467.
4. Tom Wright, *John for Everyone: Part 2, Chapters 11–21* (London: SPCK, 2002), 42–45.
5. Julian of Norwich, *Revelations of Divine Love* (New York: Penguin, 1998 trans. Elizabeth Spearing).
6. Miklos Nyiszli, *I Was Doctor Mengele's Assistant: The Memoirs of an Auschwitz Physician* (Oswiecim: Frap-Books, 2000).
7. Ibid., 141.
8. *Terror Haza: Andrassy Ut 60, House of Terror*. Official guide to the Terror Museum, Budapest, Hungary, 30.
9. The Stations of the Cross is a traditional devotion using fourteen representations of events leading up to Christ's crucifixion. These include, among others, his arrest, meeting his mother and the women of Jerusalem, several falls while carrying the cross, the crucifixion itself and the burial.
10. Tom Wright, *Luke For Everyone* (Louisville: Westminster John Knox, 2004), 138.
11. Celano, *Second Life*, in *St. Francis of Assisi: Omnibus of Sources*, 465.